Not Funny
The Soul Behind Joel

Told by Joel Richardson

Written by Lu

Joel Richardson and Lu

Copyright © 2024 Joel Richardson and Lu

All rights reserved.

ISBN: 9798878110839

Authors' Dedications

This is dedicated to my entire family. Without their support and guidance, I wouldn't be where I am today. - Joel

For my Smallie. You are everything. I couldn't have done it without you. Your turn. - Mom

Joel Richardson and Lu

CONTENTS

Forward		7
CHAPTER 1	Soul Joel	9
CHAPTER 2	Not Funny	28
CHAPTER 3	Inside Screens to Outdoor Dreams	44
CHAPTER 4	No Train, No Gain	59
CHAPTER 5	Family	72
CHAPTER 6	Welcome to the Thunder and Lighting, Snow and Rain and Hurricane Dome	105
CHAPTER 7	Leaving Rofo	117
CHAPTER 8	SunnyBrook	127
CHAPTER 9	Laying the Foundation	139
CHAPTER 10	Last, but Not Ceased	148

Joel Richardson and Lu

FORWARD by Yannis Pappas

Soul Joel embodies what stand-up comedy is all about. There is no predefined path; you must create it. You have to kill what you hunt. It takes a dreamer and adrenaline junkie. Stand-up is born in bars, banquet halls, restaurants, and hotel ballrooms – you name it, Soul Joel found a way to produce a comedy show there. Before anyone would book us, Soul Joel believed in us, and created opportunities for us to perform. Wherever Soul Joel organized a comedy event, I performed. I learned the art of stand-up comedy through Soul Joel Productions.

In the beginning, we drove 12 hours, 20 hours, for almost no money to forge a path together. They are some of the best memories of my life. Seeing Joel open his own venue fills me with joy. I owe who I am today as a stand-up comedian to Soul Joel. Joel makes it happen.

Joel Richardson and Lu

Chapter One – Soul Joel

Growing up, I'd always been goal oriented. Around age 18, my plans were not to only graduate college, but to be married and have kids by 25. Deciding on business as my major, I chose Wagner College, in Staten Island, New York City. As they say, "If you can make it there, you can make it anywhere". In 2002, I earned my bachelor's degree in marketing, from Wagner College, with a 2.47 GPA (that number will come into play later). As of now, I am single with no children of my own, but I get the pleasure of being a fun uncle to my 13 nieces and nephews. Some goals are detoured, paving the way for ones you didn't even know you had yet.

Despite having many highs and successes in life, I would accumulate a couple of chips on my shoulder. In the end, they proved to be motivators. Coming out of college, I wanted to work in pharmaceutical sales. No one would hire me because they wanted someone with a sales background, a Catch 22 situation. Having to support myself, I worked various jobs, one being with a friend from Wagner. This friend laid me off one week shy of being eligible for unemployment. It taught me a lifelong lesson; although we were friends, business is business. Friendship can be a paycheck away. Chip one. When I told my mom I got laid off, she was relieved. "Great, you weren't happy, and you just got a call from a recruiter!" Turns out, I hadn't taken my resume offline. Within two weeks, I nailed an interview and a job with Cintas in outside sales.

After a year and a half of great success with Cintas, I started getting recruited and setting up interviews with many other large pharmaceutical companies, one of them being GlaxoSmithKline. I found out that from a thousand interviewees, I was one of six potential candidates left. In the end, I didn't get the job. The managers felt that I wouldn't be able to speak eloquently to the doctors and other potential remaining candidates because I had used the words 'dude' and 'pissed'. Not exactly on Carlin's seven-words-you-can't-say list. I am originally from New Jersey, and most recently trained with Cintas, a blue-collar organization. 'Dude' was part of everyone's vocabulary, so being rejected from GSK for something as simple as two harmless words taught me that I needed to adapt quickly for the next job opportunity. Chip two.

The next interview I had was with Fauster Labossiere, my future boss at Schering-Plough. I started working with them in March of 2004, two months ahead of my two-year goal, post-graduation. Time to set a new goal. I was going to get my MBA within five years of graduating college. In 2005, one year after starting in pharma sales with Schering-Plough, I enrolled in the two-year MBA program at Wagner College full-time. This would prepare me to work my way up the corporate ladder, become a manager, and in the end, retire from pharmaceutical sales. I couldn't have been more wrong.

When I first decided to go back to school and get my MBA, the head of the program, Dr. Donald Crooks, became a mentor of mine. He was a fraternity brother at Delta Nu. Dr. Crooks knew I was better than the 2.47 GPA I had earned previously. He asked why I had gotten such low grades in my undergrad and, being completely honest, I confessed to him that I had been working and going to school both full-time and wasn't completely focused. Here comes chip three. There was a professor in the business department at Wagner, when I was getting my undergraduate degree. She oversaw the MBA program and didn't want to accept me in, stating that she felt as though I couldn't handle education at a higher level.

Ultimately, Dr. Crooks went to bat for me, and I got in, on probation. In a series of events, things were coming together that would change my life both personally and professionally. After that first year, I earned a 3.5 GPA, a full point higher than in undergrad. I would keep that GPA until I graduated in 2007, attaining the goal of getting my Master of Business Administration with a concentration in management, within that five-year goal. Wagner College, through the MBA program, gave me the foundation and education that I would need for running my own company in the future. More importantly, it helped shape my attitude and persistent mindset.

So, how did I go from slinging drugs in Brooklyn to selling jokes? Why would anyone do that, would be the smart question. Going from a very nice, steady paycheck at a job where I was almost guaranteed to move up the ranks, to doing stand-up comedy, wasn't a lateral move. It was a mudslide move. But, after being told time and time again, whether it was in class or during any one of those dreaded, three-day-long sales conferences at Schering-Plough, that I had brought joy and laughter and people looked forward to me being in the room, I was inspired. Being a bright spot in their day made the fire of making people happy within me burn brighter.

Another one of my goals is to visit all 50 states, and to date, I've been to 39. The rule is that I must sit down and enjoy a meal, it can't be a drive through or a fly over. In 1999, after my freshman year in college, I went on a road trip with my roommate, Andrew Whitman. We are from the same hometown and graduated high school together.

Our first stop was to the University of Tennessee in Knoxville, to visit his brother. After spending a few nights there, we headed to Nashville, where his dad was living. His brother surprised us with tickets to see George Carlin at the Grand Ole Opry. It was my first ever live stand-up comedy show. I don't remember who opened, if there was anyone, but I do remember George Carlin killing for over an hour. At the end of his set, Carlin acknowledges playing in the Bible Belt and proclaims, "If there is a God, let me get struck by lightning right here and now." Ten, nine, eight... he starts a countdown, gets to zero, and defiantly snarks, "Look, see?" Literally over a thousand people started getting up and walking out. Murmurs of disapproval and disgust filled the arena. George ends with, "And that's my time." and walks off stage. It was the first time I realized there were two shows going on: one for the audience, and one for the comics.

In the fall of that same year, I was on a double date with one of my Delta Nu brothers, Mike Ponzo. After dinner, we stumbled upon a comedy club in Greenwich Village. I'm still riding high from seeing George Carlin five months ago, so of course I was willing to check this place out. Not realizing I was headed into one of the best, most famous comedy clubs in the country, we headed down the steps of The Comedy Cellar. That night's line-up included Wanda Sykes, Lisa Lampanelli, Dave Attell, Greg Giraldo, Louis CK, and Keith Robinson. Keith was hosting, and halfway through the show he mentions, "You've been a good crowd, please welcome special guest Chris Rock." Chris Rock walks in and I'm 10 feet from him doing his set. I was like, man, this is what New York's all about. From that point on, I was hooked. I caught the comedy bug and made it a point to attend at least one comedy show per month for the foreseeable future.

On May 29, 2006, I started my journey in comedy. Halfway through the MBA program, to kick off the summer, some classmates and I decided to attend our first open mic. Two of us decided to sign up and perform. My first open mic was at Martini Red, a small bar in Staten Island, with a performance space in the back. Shows there were 'open stage', which means a mix of comics and musicians. Being on that stage for 10 minutes, which I had no business being on stage for 10 whole minutes as a new comic, I realized my life was changed forever. It was almost like trading one drug for another. That adrenaline rush from making people laugh, I never wanted to give that up. The first time a wave of laughter filled the room because of me and my jokes was like nothing I had ever experienced.

New comics need to do open mics and what they call 'bringer shows', where you bring people to your shows to help fill the seats, to get stage time. I did every contest. I handed out flyers in Greenwich Village in New York City. I did everything imaginable, just to get stage time. It was brutal.

After a year, I was signed up to do a show in Central New Jersey, not far from Staten Island. At 2:00pm that day, a Saturday, the **DJ/promoter** called me up with a lame excuse about how there were two owners and one of them signed off, but the other one didn't. The show was canceled, and although it wasn't my fault, I felt totally responsible. Chip four. I had 30 people coming to that show and six hours to let them know it wasn't happening. I didn't have everyone's phone numbers and scrambled to contact them via Facebook and MySpace. This was a definite turning point. I knew then, I had to start putting together my own shows, creating my own opportunities and taking control of events that would shape my own path and ultimately my career, in order to make all my hard work pay off. Always having been the friend who organized events, whether it was a school reunion or a bachelor party, I took my skill set and passion and applied it to comedy.

The first event I organized was a $20, two-hour, all-you-can-drink comedy show. One hundred percent of the money went to the owner of Rudy and Deans, a second-story bar on Staten Island, overlooking the Manhattan skyline. I made no money from it, but knew if I made it an open bar, people would come. Butts-in-the-seats leads to word-of-mouth promotion.

It was a wild night. My Aunt Patti Jo had driven my grandmother all the way from Uniontown in Western Pennsylvania. Patti Jo wanted to take advantage of the open bar, so she would pound a Coors Light before walking back to the table with another. She didn't want my grandmother to know how much she was drinking. My sister, Deanna, came too. I can still hear the clunking of her heels as she was falling down the flight of stairs, and my Delta Nu brother, Chris Gerlach, pointing out, "Joel's sister, shocker!" Heels and an open bar do not mix. One of the comics, Dave Zdanowitz, who I met at the Stress Factory in New Jersey, got so drunk before the show that he fell over the stage while being introduced and never recovered. All-you-can-drink leads to butts on the floor. Besides Dave, I lined up Greg Mescal, a fellow Wagner College MBA Program alumnus, who is currently announcing for

ESPN covering the United States Women's Polo team, and Gaetano Barbuto, my friend since kindergarten, who both did well that night. I'm the only one still performing.

My run at Ruddy and Deans only lasted for two shows, probably because the second show ended in a verbal confrontation with the owner punching me in the face. All I remember was waking up on the floor with my cheek black and blue. The timing was impeccable. I was still working at Schering-Plough and was scheduled for a monthly ride-along with my manager, Fauster Labossiere. Here I was, with a yellowish, fading bruised face from a bar fight, or sucker punch as I recall, having to explain to my boss what happened without looking like a maniac. I told him I was dribbling a basketball and it hit my face. Looking uncoordinated was better than looking unruly.

I knew hooks. I knew how to 'bring 'em out'. I knew showmanship. It was only a matter of time until I, myself, became a brand. In the summer of 2006, I was doing a lot of open mics. One, in particular, birthed what is now my trademark and my legacy. At The Stress Factory in New Jersey, I was one of 30 to 40 open micers. My last name is Richardson - not a particularly hard name to pronounce, but it's long. The host that night announced, "Keep it going for the next comic, Joel Richards!" Up to this point, I had heard that many times, but on this night, it hit me; I needed to separate myself from all the other white male comics, as to not get lost in the crowd. I needed the crowd to remember my name, not just my jokes. So many times, people would comment, "That last comic was funny, what's their name?" How could I change that? In high school, I was tagged 'SoulJoel' because of the dances I would do after I scored a goal in soccer. *C'mon n' Ride It (The Train)* by Quad City DJ's was my dance of choice and I stand behind it! Listen, it was very popular at the time, 1996, and I rocked it, to my recollection anyway. I didn't score very often, thankfully some would say. One of my teammates was like, "Why you always dancing, Soul Joel?" and it just kinda stuck.

"Keep throwing darts, eventually you'll hit the bullseye." 'SoulJoel' is the bullseye, but 'Far Running Fat Man' was the first dart. Matt Friedman, a friend I met at Wagner, wisecracked, "You really are a far running fat man." after finding out I had just completed my first marathon. I considered using it as my comic name. I went as far as using that name to head a blogging website for four years, having over 20 bloggers at its peak. I had been known for running so much, that my friend, Tom Shekker, who worked for Dunkin', asked me to run as Cuppy, the Dunkin' mascot, for The Broad Street Run in Philadelphia. I couldn't commit fast enough. Joel runs on Dunkin'. On race day, as I was coming out of the subway station in full costume, making my way to the starting line, a man glanced at me and shouts, "Now YOU know you're getting on TV rocking that!" He was right, any station covering that race had my Cuppy runnething over Broad Street. When I eventually went from Joel Richardson to SoulJoel, I got the same reaction as Prince changing his name to ☿. It was the laughingstock of the New York comedy scene until I finally established my brand years later.

One night, I was on a show in the basement of Gotham Comedy Club, in their smaller lounge. Kunal Arora was closing it out. We had never met, and Kunal arrived after the show started, so he missed my spot. Two of my Delta Nu fraternity brothers, AJ Palumbo and Justin Brenner, had shown up in their original, decade old, SOUL shirts to support me. Just before Kunal goes on stage, he comes over and asks me if anyone on the show had addressed the two guys wearing SOUL shirts yet? I told him no one had, and they were fair game. He goes up and does what he does best, improving most of his set. There were only 20 people in the crowd, eight that knew Kunal personally, and my two college friends, making up 50% of the audience. He went on to make fun of the fact that the shirts only read 'SOUL' across the front. I think if this had happened years earlier, I might have questioned my own branding more. My approach to comedy and my branding had changed from only wanting to perform to being a full-time comedy producer, in order to make a living.

That same night, as the show was ending, we got word that Jerry Seinfeld was on his way to perform upstairs on the main stage. As soon as I walked up stairs, Jerry was walking in with his Mets hat pulled down over his eyes and his set list in hand. I was amazed to see a veteran like Jerry approach his set the same way after all these years, holding a list of material he wanted to work out. The minute Jerry got on stage, he took off his hat and looked at the crowd with both hands extended to the side as if to say, "Can you believe it?" The crowd went bananas, magic filled the air. This was what comedy in New York City was all about.

My second Seinfeld sighting was in Vegas. One of my fraternity brothers, Mike Fish, got married there during the Summer of 2007. Mike Ponzo, Billy Eisenbraun, their wives, and I flew out for the wedding. After the ceremony, we went out to eat at Rao in Ceasar's Palace. Minutes after we got our table, Jerry Seinfeld comes and sits at the table next to ours. He was with Tom Papa, who was opening for him, and some other folks. Throughout the 90 minutes it took to eat, there must have been 30 or more people who approached Jerry to ask him questions, each time interrupting his meal or conversation with the others at his table. Many of the questions were about 'George' and 'Kramer', not even the real actors. No one in our group said a word, we were from New York, we minded our own business. I had learned this lesson early on in comedy. I knew there was nothing you could say to someone at Jerry Seinfeld's level that hasn't been said to him before. The cool part of the night was after dinner. Our group played bocce ball in the courtyard of Rao, while Jerry and Tom smoked cigars at a nearby table. It certainly added some memorable moments to that trip.

I ended up meeting Tom Shekker through Pete Kingston, one of my best friends since kindergarten. Pete's older brother, Jeff, was the Director of Baseball Operations for the San Diego Padres, at the time, and we would go to their spring training every year in Scottsdale, Arizona. Jeff is now the Assistant General Manager of the Los Angeles Dodgers, with a World Series ring on his resume! Back in Arizona, I met Mike Cameron, along with many other Padres players. My confidence was shining, and I'm not sure why, but I decided to vocalize it by telling Mike that one day, "I would be more famous than he is." Perfect timing, as Mike was just coming off of earning multiple gold gloves and an all-star appearance, along with a previous World Series appearance with the Mets. Not to mention, Mike had just signed a 19.5-million-dollar contract and I had just completed my tenth open mic. There's still time.

In addition to pursuing stage time in 2007, I started producing shows. Within months, I created my own comedy circuit. I set up regular shows, some quarterly and some monthly, where others and I would perform. One of the first places to pay me a budget was Madd Anthony's. Their address was 'two and a quarter miles south of the Pocono Raceway'. Seriously. I guess I'm lucky it said south and not 'as the crow flies'. In my first year at Madd Anthony's, the headliners were DJ Hazzard, the first person I ever opened for, Julian McCullough, Yannis Pappas, and Nate Bargatze. I had known Julian since middle school and had met Yannis and Nate through other comedians. My first paid gig, where I opened for DJ Hazzard, was on someone else's show. It was a five-hour, round-trip drive from New York to Hazleton, PA, where I banked $50. It wasn't a lot, but it was truly worth it. Anything to build on experience was worth it.

One of the shows at Madd Anthony's with Nate Bargatze was quite memorable. We were there with John Szeluga, who is now a writer/producer for the Impractical Jokers, and another comedian, Pat O'Shea. Most of the shows I produced in the first two or three years, I offered the comedians rides. It was part of the deal, so they wouldn't have to pay for gas and tolls. Sometimes the car rides would be as funny as the shows on stage.

We had all driven to Madd Anthony's, a bar/pizzeria, together. Most of the patrons had been drinking since they had gotten off work hours before and were not there to hear us joke about sleeping till noon and banging the bar leftovers. In fact, just recently, on my podcast *Bring 'Em Out!* with co-host Alan Hill, John made me aware of one such patron. Unbeknownst to me, John was warned right before the show not to mess with a certain individual. The last time someone did, the guy left, came back with a shotgun, and blasted a hole in the ceiling! In case you missed it, he was warned that night because the guy WAS THERE that night. John goes on to tell us that at the end of the night, the guy came up to the table where all the comics were sitting and bellowed, "You boys all sucked tonight. Let me buy you a drink." Isn't that the most Pennsylvania thing? They might be animals, but they're kind. Eagles fans, I'm looking at you.

So, Pat was on stage, doing a bit that used the line "Shut up Leon, just shut up!" from a movie. Instantly, a guy at the bar shouts out, "That's a great idea! Why don't you shut the fuck up?!" There is nothing worse for a comedian to hear, spoken word is all we have. **If comics shut up, we would be mimes, and no one invites a mime into their life.** Turned out this heckle ended up being a two-fer. On our way back to New York, Nate was riding shotgun, Pat and John were in the back, and I was driving, of course. Nate's phone had died, so he asked to borrow mine. I had no idea who he was texting at the time.

As we passed over the PA/NJ border, Nate reached for the radio and asked if everyone liked rock. We all replied we did, and he turned on 92.3 K-ROCK in New York, the station Howard Stern left before going to Sirius. As soon as he turns up the volume, the DJ coming out of the commercial announces, "This is Dan Soder on 92.3 K-ROCK, and that was "Enter Sandman" by Metallica. We just got word that SoulJoel Productions rocked out in the Poconos and is heading back to New York City. And by the way, shut up Pat, just shut up!" Dan is now known for his role on Showtime's *Billions*, formerly cohosting *The Bonfire* with Big Jay Oakerson on SiriusXM, numerous TV and podcast appearances, along with several specials, and is currently touring and hosting his own podcast *Soder*.

    I immediately looked in the rear-view mirror where John and Pat were staring at us, as Nate burst out laughing. Pat was so confused at first. He thought he was listening to some sort of commercial that I paid for, then he thought he bombed so hard that news had hit New York and people were already talking about it. Quickly, he came to his senses and realized it was all a practical joke by Nate. Comedy gig road trips are legendary, good or bad, cathartic or crazy, but always legendary.

    As I think back, every story I remember seems to branch off into another unrelated story that makes me laugh and I have to share, like just now. As I was picturing Nate's antics in the last paragraph, I was reminded of when he and I did a gig in Uniontown. We had just finished, and I was packing up my sound equipment. As I was walking back to do one last sweep of the place, I bumped into Nate, who was holding my joke book, a journal full of all my jokes. In true Nate fashion, with his dry delivery, he nonchalantly jokes, "I was gonna throw this out, but I figured you'd want to do it." Gotta love him.

In 2008, my roommate, Scott Chamberlin, and I started SoulJoel Productions. Within three years, we set up shows in 14 different states. To date, we have run shows in over 22. In the same year, we launched The Staten Island Comedy Festival. This seven-day, seven different venues event, for seven different charities, included the likes of: Colin Jost, Casey Jost, Sal Vulcano, Gary Gulman, Otto and George, Mick Foley, Artie Lange, Judah Friedlander, Bonnie McFarlane, Sherrod Small, Pete Davidson, and Vic Dibitetto, among others.

Funny side note: shortly after creating the festival, I met a very young Pete Davidson and put him on stage for the first time, three weeks before his 16th birthday. Whenever we would do shows together, I'd have to carry a permission slip, from his mom, in the car because I was transporting a minor across state lines. Years later, after he was managed by Nick Cannon, he called me up. I had booked him a show in New Jersey to headline for me, for the first time. "I hope you're not mad at me, but I have a meeting with Lorne Michaels, and I can't do the show at Lefty's Tavern in New Jersey." Of course, my first reaction was, not only was it a bigger opportunity for him, but he may get paid *a little bit* more by NBC and Lorne Michaels, than I can pay him to headline in the back of a restaurant in New Jersey. That next week, they announced Pete Davidson as the youngest cast member of *SNL* since Adam Sandler and Eddie Murphy. A bunch of people started messaging me, because they had seen Pete on my shows. It was success by association.

Not Funny – The Soul Behind Joel

Chapter Two – Not Funny

Although things were going well in New York, something was pulling me towards Pennsylvania. In 2019, I had a meeting with Boyd Entertainment, who had just bought the Valley Forge Casino from an investment group, which, from their inception, had hired me to do shows. Over the seven years I worked for them, I did a show once a month for the first five years, and, after building a following, was consistently booked every Friday for the last two. After Boyd took over, someone from management, let's call her 'Tina', offered me Thursday nights. Right away I thought, "Great!", they were adding an additional night. Instead, I found out they were replacing my regular Friday shows with Dueling Pianos. As you can imagine, this switch was completely deflating, letting me know that I was not appreciated there. After the owners that I had been working for decided to sell the casino, it became clear to me that it was an 'out with the old and in with the new' situation, and I was part of the old. Chip five.

That year, I resolved to finally leave the comfort zone of steady work in Valley Forge, spread my wings, and open SoulJoel's in Royersford, PA. Although only ten miles away, it was ten minutes further west in uncharted territory for myself and my production company. I chose Royersford because of Brian Flammer, certainly not because it was an easy town to pronounce. Brian, my biggest fan at the time, was from Royersford and had posted something on a local community group Facebook page, polling people on how they'd feel about a comedy club coming to their town. In 24 hours, it had over 300 positive comments. I quickly asked Brian to delete the post, not wanting any parallel thinking. After Brian introduced me to the 'powers that be' in town, we found a place to set up shop. It wasn't a quick transaction, it took months, but eventually the first iteration of what is now known as SoulJoel's was born.

While producing my own shows over the years, I saw many comedians, quote unquote, make it. Going along this journey, the definition of 'making it' certainly changes. Getting on *The Tonight Show*, having a special on Comedy Central, and touring in stadiums were the pinnacle of stand-up success. Now, it can be seen as having millions of followers on Instagram doing crowd work clips. Giving me something to aspire to my close friend, Julian McCullough, passed at The Comedy Cellar, the mecca of making it in the New York stand-up world. I was like, wow, man he's blowing up. Later, he would become the warm-up comedian for *The Colbert Report* on Comedy Central, get his own special, become a regular on *Guy Code* on MTV, have a show with Whitney Cummings on E!, and eventually move to California. I was just so happy for someone I grew up with and continue to call a friend. Witnessing many of my friends succeed by achieving their dreams continues to be inspirational and a genuine joy for me.

In fact, back in December of 2006, I was privileged to witness the rise of a real 'up-and-comer', or so I thought. I was six months into comedy and at home visiting my family for Christmas break. I decided to attend my first open mic at The Laff House in Philadelphia. The club is no longer there, but had given birth to many Philly comedians, including Kevin Hart.

Just after I got off stage, the host of the open mic, The Legendary Wid, introduced Keith Robinson. He goes on for thirty minutes and completely destroys, as only Keith can do. Filled with liquid courage, I approached Keith and Rod, the owner of the Laff House, sitting at the bar in the club's lobby. Unsolicited, I told Keith, "Hang in there, you're right there! You're going to make it soon and blow up." Keith's response, "You hear that, Rod? This young boy says all I have to do is hang in there." Keith, at the time, had more television appearances than I had been on stage. He was an established full-time comic at The Comedy Cellar. He had been a regular on *Tough Crowd* with Colin Quinn. He, by anyone's definition, had already "made it". I had no business dropping that pearl of wisdom onto Keith. In my mind, I was being encouraging, but my state of mind was more than slightly altered.

After creating SoulJoel Productions, I, along with Yannis Pappas and James Mattern, kicked off The SoulJoel Family Tour in 2008. We set up shows in every place I knew where my family lived close by, including western Pennsylvania, outside of Pittsburgh, Uniontown, South Jersey, and, obviously, Staten Island, where I was living at the time.

On May 6, 2009, the three of us were in my car on the way back from Uniontown, my father's hometown, also where all four of my grandparents went to high school. It was a special place for my family. I determined on that car ride to commit to giving everything I had and focusing on SoulJoel Productions full-time. Although it was scary, they both agreed and encouraged me, declaring that it was the best thing I could do and the perfect time to do it. Yannis confided in me. He basically said, "If you focus on being a comedian, you're funny enough to be a decent middle act or feature. But you were given the ability to produce and be the best that ever lived. Why not embrace that?"

At that moment, although he said I was funny enough, it made me feel not funny. That honesty from a friend, the type of friend that everyone needs, someone who isn't afraid to tell you the truth if it will help you see the truth you're missing, was the catalyst I needed. I wasn't going to make a living as a middle, I was going to prosper knowing and promoting funny. Combining my MBA in management with an undergraduate degree in marketing and my experience and love for comedy, I was set to rule the world, or the Tri-state area, at least.

Speaking of car rides to and from gigs, they were often more memorable than the actual shows we were traveling to. Comedians live in their cars or on airplanes, especially in the beginning of their careers. The first car I owned after quitting pharmaceutical sales was dubbed the 'SoulJoel Mobile'. It was a Chevy HHR that racked up 119,000 miles in two and a half years.

I remember being in the car with Kurt Metzger and James Mattern. I'd known Kurt and James for about four or five years at this point. James was going by the name of Mad Dog Mattern and I, of course, was SoulJoel. Kurt asked what

James's real name was and recommended we both go by our real names. Although Kurt was right, Joel Richardson was better for business, 'SoulJoel' had a snappy appeal and I kept it. James eventually went back to James Mattern. I've gotten a lot of heat and made fun of countless times by some of the biggest acts in the country for the SoulJoel name, but I knew if I stuck to my brand and my plan, it would all pay off.

As part of the Southern States Tour with James Mattern, Yannis Pappas, Scott Chamberlin, and myself, we headed to Boca Raton, Savannah, and Charleston, in that order. We drove from southern Florida back up to Georgia through South Carolina, realizing afterward that those stops should have been a little bit closer to each other. (Years later I would discover that the route we took wasn't ideal. Hey, what can I say? GPS wasn't as popular then!)

Every show, every stop, was a future lesson in running my own club, what to do, and most importantly, what not to do. Each leg of this trip, we would get there early, so I could hit the streets and hand out fliers. Guerrilla marketing seemed the only way to succeed. Quickly, I found out that The New York Comedy Club, now known as The Boca Black Box, was consistently handing out comp tickets to their shows, specifically while we were in town. Most people I handed a flier to would respond with, "Why would I pay for tickets to that club when I can get them for free (from The New York Comedy Club)?"

In Savannah, I would learn a different lesson. On the third day of barking (passing out flyers for a comedy show in the streets), I got called out by the police. To this point, they had assumed I was passing out religious literature, which were the only legal pamphlets allowed. I had been wearing a shirt with the word SOUL emblazoned on the front, a well-worn, signature shirt of mine. While there, I also got spotted wearing that shirt by a fellow Wagner College alumni and fraternity brother, Jeremiah Jarmin. He was in Savannah for a wedding, and we ended up hanging out. It's just so funny how big the world is but ends up being so small... and possibly I need to get some new shirts.

Jumping to 2017, I would launch *The Comedy Point* podcast, in a studio I devised out of my house. Ultimately, this transitioned into the start of SoulJoel TV, where we continue to create content through videos, sketches, and a podcast network to this day. I originally started *The Comedy Point* podcast eight years prior, in Warwick, NY on AM and FM radio, where I would upload it as a podcast and make it available anywhere podcasts were available.

This time around, my co-hosts would be comedian Mark Riccadonna, Geno Vento of Geno's Steak's in South Philly, and Chuck Gill, a real bearded Santa for the Philly Pops, my 4th grade teacher and the first manager at Sunnybrook Swim Club, where I was a lifeguard in my teens. Through this podcast I would meet many people that would become family, including Tony Luke Jr. of Tony Luke's in Philly, and Troy Hendrickson, the creator of Aunt Mary Pat. I began booking Aunt Mary Pat after Geno introduced us. Troy texted me one day asking if I knew anyone who would want to manage him. "Yeah, me!" I suggested. We worked together to elevate the Aunt Mary Pat brand from regional to a nationally touring act. To this day, I continue to manage her, and she continues to crush.

Being around Geno Vento, an icon of Philadelphia, I got a taste of what it was like to be internationally known, while being a good businessman and remaining humble. For these lessons, among others, I'm forever grateful. Geno even resuscitated my days as a running mascot. After telling him I ran as Cuppy, he proposed I run as Wizzy, the mascot for Geno's, the following year. Before you know it, Geno had the costume made and asked me to help with his press tour. Wizzy was the first cheesesteak mascot in Philadelphia. We visited schools, the famous steps in front of the Philadelphia Museum of Arts (made famous by the Rocky movies), cheered on the Temple Owls, and were featured on *Good Day Philadelphia* on Fox29. I ended up having to pause this version of my podcast in 2020 because SoulJoel's was starting up, and it became too much.

Things were moving forward. In order to make my business plan of opening a club work, I needed a space that could occupy 200 to 250 people, bare minimum. I visited a couple of potential spots, but to no avail. Either they weren't big enough or it wasn't feasible. After inspecting the latest unsatisfactory building, the landlord informed me that this was the last piece of property left in Royersford. Under no circumstances did I believe that, and I confronted the borough with the news. After informing them that I appreciated their time, I began looking for a building elsewhere. I wasn't going to try and fit a square peg into a round hole. I was advised to contact Rick Lewis of Lewis Environmental. We connected and he loved my plan of bringing a comedy club to town. He was already planning a business riverfront along the Schuylkill River, and SoulJoel's would fit right in.

There, on the third floor of an old stove factory, I would rent a space, with plans of quickly expanding into a larger room in the foundry on the other side of the building. Rick was completely supportive of bringing attention to his riverfront project and to Royersford. November 1, 2019, would be my first show, starring Vic Henely as the headliner. We sold out well in advance. It was the highest of highs.

After selling out that first night, I was ecstatic with my new home. Even though capacity was only 150, I was looking forward to moving on up to the bigger space. For now, I was going to make this room work. Then came week two and three, each claiming only half capacity. Boy, was that humbling. It left me wondering if moving my operation ten minutes west of Philadelphia and even farther from New York City was a good idea. I started second guessing everything.

During week number two, comedians Dennis Rooney and Chris Roach, who I had known for years, were at the club. Both these guys were very good friends of mine. We were so close in fact, had I ever gotten married, they would have been invited. I not only booked great talent, but great friends that were good people. I walked into the green room just before the show. Dennis scans me up and down, "Dude, is it just a two man show?" Fluctuating between club owner and comedian, I hadn't quite figured out which look goes with what job, and I was on the dais that night. His question was referring to the very dapper outfit I was wearing; dress pants and a blazer, more something a club owner would wear, than a stand-up comic. Dennis felt I looked too good to be a comedian, or maybe he was hoping I wasn't on the show! Either way it made the entire green room laugh.

SoulJoel's was open one day a week, for the first four weeks. Thanksgiving fell during that fourth week and Joe DeRosa headlined Wednesday, Friday, and Saturday. It was amazing. We started to gain traction again. In December of 2019, we set out to add fundraisers on Thursday nights, helping to round out the weekend. Our first fundraiser was for Spring-Ford SNAP, and it was a huge success. I'm extremely proud to announce, to date, SoulJoel's has helped raise close to $85,000 for various charities, half of which was raised during the pandemic.

Six weeks after our grand opening, Aunt Mary Pat was the first artist to sell out a full weekend of shows. The weekend before Christmas, she packed two shows Friday and two shows Saturday, attracting 600 people in 48 hours. I remember two men in line with their wives, buying merch and doing the meet and greet with Aunt Mary Pat. They were talking about how each of them had heard about SoulJoel's. It was because of Aunt Mary Pat. She was instrumental in boosting the club's recognition. Within four months, we went from being open one day a week to being open five days a week. Monday was open mic night, special shows were scheduled on Wednesdays, Thursdays hosted charity events, and Fridays-Saturdays were for traditional stand-up. The turnaround was astonishing.

Not Funny – The Soul Behind Joel

When I talk about SoulJoel's, I often refer to 'we', because I could not have realized my dream without help along the way. Thinking back to when I left the Valley Forge Casino, one person comes to mind straightaway – Joey St. John. When I was saying my goodbyes there, I wanted to especially thank Joey for all the incredible work he had done as a videographer and social media manager. I told him about opening my own club and he quickly proposed, "I don't know what we have to do to make this happen, but please take me with you." Absolutely. I valued his abilities and knew he'd be an asset.

At first, I hired him part-time, making videos and graphics. By December he was needed full-time, as the club was taking off. I was still producing shows in other states, so his help was invaluable and trusting him was a load off my mind, one less stress. During this time, I'd travel to Florida managing shows with Shuli Egar, writer and producer for the Stern Show. We set up a week's worth of shows for Aunt Mary Pat, while running monthly satellite shows at the Robin's Nest in Mount Holly, NJ (a place I waited tables years ago), Octoraro's in Oxford, PA, and Harbor Square Theater in Stone Harbor, NJ.

Our first New Year's Eve was very memorable. As I arrived early at the club that night, I noticed three Royersford police cars parked in the lot. First thing that popped into my mind was that someone is going to get a DUI leaving the show after the ball drops at midnight. I parked my car and got a text from Joe Chip, a friend from South Jersey, who was coming to sing and play acoustic guitar before and after the comedy show. His message read that he had a funny story for me. Joe had trouble seeing at night and after his GPS instructed him to make a right-hand turn, did so instantaneously, not realizing he did it too soon and drove over train tracks, getting stuck. That's why the police were called, to help him get off the tracks. This wouldn't be the last time the Reading Railroad derailed a show at SoulJoel's.

Because the club was picking up steam, and I was going back and forth between states, I offered Joey a one-year contract. I would be paying him for an entire year, that was a promise I made. Meanwhile, at the end of February, Chuck Nice performed for our second sold out weekend, four shows total. Chuck went on *The John DeBella Show*, a morning show on 102.9 WMGK out of Philadelphia, to promote. DeBella is a radio legend, having been on the air for almost five decades. Chuck also made an appearance on Fox 29's *Good Day Philadelphia*, plugging his upcoming shows. All this press was bolstering our recognizability.

Two weeks later, I had booked my friend Julian McCullough. Jullian flew in from LA to do a show in our hometown, Moorestown, that Thursday, then two shows in Royersford, Friday and Saturday. I'll never forget when Julian got off the plane and into my car. He asked, "What's up, buddy?" I responded, "I think you're getting back on that plane, that's what's up." In that short, five-hour, cross country flight, the nation was being shut down due to COVID-19. It happened differently in each state and region of the country, but Pennsylvania was one of the first to enforce the shutdown of nonessential activity. Simultaneously, Joey was overseeing the Thursday fundraiser in Royersford. Those two shows ended up being the last we would do for a while. Thursday, March 12, 2020, the government shutdowns started going into effect and comedy shows were deemed non-essential. Jullian flew home the next day. No shows = no money coming in = now what?

It was a roller coaster. Just as we were really taking off, it felt like we plummeted to a complete stop. I, like the rest of the world, was left wondering what would happen next. I came too far to let this thing die. I needed to figure out my next move. People in the comedy business were desperately trying anything. Stand-ups were going live on various social media outlets. I respected the hustle, but there isn't the same connection online as there is with an in-person audience. Things were looking bleak. In April of 2020, I went to bed with $300 in my bank account. The next day payroll was due. I did not know how I was going to keep my promise to Joey. We were only five months into our contract.

Miraculously, the next day, I woke up to the first government grant automatically deposited into my bank account. It was enough to cover what I owed Joey, with money left over. I did not take this grant for granted, especially now knowing that a lot of businesses closed during this time. The shift in energy was palpable. The universe was telling me I was on the right path. This was supposed to happen.

Not Funny – The Soul Behind Joel

Chapter Three – Inside Screens to Outside Dreams

When certain people call, you always pick up the phone. In today's world with Facebook and Instagram, social media in general, it's easier to text someone, but the old school call, to me, is personal and means it's more important. Fellow small business owner, Mike McCluskey, who had been one of my biggest supporters since opening in Royersford, called me late April of 2020. He suggested doing an outside show in May. It could be socially distant, everyone would wear masks, and can be safe. In my head I was thinking, man, outdoor comedy doesn't really work, but what was the alternative?

The government was shutting down businesses left and right because of strict restrictions on large gatherings due to the worldwide pandemic. Inside comedy shows were banned for who knows how long. I had seen people attempt to do stand-up shows live over the computer, but stand-up comedy doesn't really translate over a screen. We even tried a few Zoom shows during the first months of the shutdown. It's bad enough to lose someone's attention in the same room, it is humiliating watching them leave the screen to get a snack over Zoom. I decided I'd roll with it.

Recruiting two comedians, Richie Byrne and Missy Hall, to co-headline, and with me hosting, I carried out my first outdoor comedy show. That show led to doing shows in various parking lots in the area, teaming up with local small businesses. We used the municipal parking lot across from Annamarie's and Salon Evolve's lot. Kim from Salon Evolve, **was very instrumental in my decision to keep BYOB as a business model, as we had done previously indoors.** The outdoor shows were: bring your own booze, your own food, your own chair...BYOBFC. Teaming up with local businesses meant our audiences would patronize them, too. SoulJoel's brought a lot of people to town. It was a win-win.

My landlord, Rick Lewis, decided to call a meeting. He wanted me to start doing shows in his outside, vacant, dirt lot, directly next to SoulJoel's indoor spot. We decided that July 3, 2020, would be our first outdoor show at that location. I called it an amphitheater. It was crazy. It was unheard of. It was nuts. On Rick's suggestion, a company close by in Spring City sold us a 40ft. tractor trailer bed. That was our stage. It sounded insane but ended up being completely brilliant.

I recalled, through our documentary (*Soul Survivor* on SoulJoelTV 's YouTube), that some comedians did not want to book shows there at first, because it looked so bad. Mike Vecchione said it best, referring to comics in general, "I don't want to be the guy who figures it out." but also noted that I (Joel) knew comedy and would figure out the right way to make it work for everyone. I believe that's why he agreed, along with Justin Silver, to take a crack at outdoor comedy with us, when, for the short time before the trailer bed, we had only a 4x4 homemade wooden platform. Justin Silver videoed the event. "This is quarantine comedy. Performing in a parking lot and it just started raining." as he turns the camera to Mike riffing on the microphone to a crowd on lawn chairs in a dirt lot. "I didn't check the weather before tonight because I never performed outside." Then Justin pans over to a lady packing up and slowly walking to her car. Talk about big dreams from humble beginnings.

After our second outdoor show in the dirt lot, a man named Gilbert Moyer came up to Joey St.

John and me wondering what our intentions were for the stage. He asked because he was a carpenter, and the comedians were making fun of the tractor trailer stage during their sets, nonstop. (Big thanks to Greg Stone and Louis Katz). Gilbert won't like this mentioned, but we called him our angel. He took two days off work to turn the trailer bed into a black box, refusing to accept any money, and simply asking us to pay for all the supplies. In the summer of 2020, because we were working outside daily, I was rocking the best tan I'd ever had in my adult life. Gilbert tried to turn a lifelong salesman and a videographer into carpenters and handymen. Gil not only wanted to help, but he also wanted to teach. Without his assistance, the stage would never have looked the way it did, so good in fact, some comedians never realized it was a flatbed.

With an idea my sister, Deanna, came up with, we covered the lot with sand. Two hundred tons and nine triaxle loads of it. Nine huge trucks dumped tons of sand over the lot where a yarn factory once stood. Most people have a 401k match program with their employers, I had a sand match program with Rick. I bought 100 tons, he matched with 100 more. With a lot of hard work, we brought the beach to landlocked Royersford. I'm forever grateful to Rick Lewis' generosity during that time. It was scary and mentally draining, but we were creating a scene that felt rock and roll, rebellious, and would end up becoming a milestone in comedy history.

Modeling The Staten Island Comedy Festival I started in 2008, I decided to put together the first SoulJoel's *SummerFest*. Seventeen straight days of performances for every week lost during the shutdown. *SummerFest* ran from July 31st to August 16, 2020. Joe List and Mark Normand were two of the first headliners. Joe had a new special coming out, called *Joe List: I Hate Myself*, around the same time. As was before with Chuck Nice, Joe went on a press tour to promote.

I was flooded with messages from excited people who had heard him on *The Preston & Steve Show* on WMMR, *Jim and Sam* on SiriusXM, and many more radio programs and podcasts, including his own, *Tuesdays with Stories!*. He really hyped us up, mentioning 'SoulJoel's! SoulJoel's! SoulJoel's!' on every show. I sent him a message thanking him, confessing I owed him a Christmas present and another gig for all this free publicity. He comes back with. "No problem, man, it's been fun. Hey, do you want Louis to play at your place?" Speechless. Do I want one of the biggest and arguably one of the best stand-ups in the world to do a set in the sand? Yes. The answer was, without question, yes.

Louis CK would appear a total of four times during the 16 months we were outside in

Royersford, from September of 2020 to April of 2021. Every time, without incident. People were starving for comedy and to be able to see a great like Louis CK in an intimate setting was a special treat.

To make *SummerFest* 2020 even more exceptional, it ended with a bang. When tickets were originally put on sale, we teased a "Special Guest Headliner" who would appear for two shows on Sunday, August 16th, capping off the festival. It was a week into the festival that we actually confirmed our headliner as none other than the legend, Dave Attell.

We weren't without a few flare ups, however. It wouldn't be a SoulJoel production without a few minor floods to overcome. On day 13, we had Yannis Pappas headlining. It had been pouring rain all day, all week for that matter, the effects of hurricanes and tropical storms in the northeast. My sister had just gotten back from buying skids of sand from Lowe's. While she was there the cashier informed her that her car would not be able to carry that big a load. Knowing that the show was set to start in an hour and a half, she had to get the sand back quickly. She saw a truck outside and asked the owner, a stranger, if he could help haul the sand. Deanna wrote the address on a piece of paper and prayed he wouldn't take off with the bags.

Thankfully, he delivered. We were covered in sand from head to toe, trying to fill in the puddles left by the storm, and here comes Yannis. As he pulls up, Yannis rolls down his window, leans out like *Dumb and Dumber*, and casually remarks, "Are you still trying to do comedy during this apocalypse, bud?" We were tired, wet, sandy, scrambling, and frustrated. I wanted to strangle him, but we couldn't help but to stop and crack up laughing. To this day, I still laugh at how ridiculous we must have looked trying to make that show happen.

While spending all this time outdoors, I ended up getting a strange bite on my left ankle. I knew right away that I needed immediate attention and went to urgent care. As I was waiting, sitting on the paper-covered exam table, the doctor walked in and recognized me. "Oh, you're Joel from SoulJoel's!" It never ceases to amaze me, being recognized in the strangest places.

She shared with me that she really enjoyed going to the comedy shows and a lot of people said the same to her, and that bringing people together through laughter was really saving people during this pandemic. A real shot in the arm. She examined the bite and prescribed medication. After a few days, I noticed the area was not getting better, but in reality, it was growing worse, with a red line starting up my leg towards my heart, so I went back. She confided to me that she didn't think it had been that serious and passed on giving me an antibiotic.

The power of celebrity had blinded her to her duties! Just joking. I got the much-needed medication and was quickly on the road to recovery.

The next day was lucky fourteen, lucky for us, anyway. The Big Jay Oakerson incident. Big Jay wasn't even supposed to be on that show. Dave Smith had been scheduled with Luis J. Gomez. On the Monday *Legion of Skanks* podcast prior, they announced Dave had a death in the family and he would not be joining Luis at SoulJoel's. They announced that the other third of LOS, Big Jay, would replace him. The show was hosted by James Mattern.

James had been living with us since the start of *SummerFest* and hosted almost every show. He may hold the record of most on stage appearances in the world over the lockdown. James Mattern on hosting that first summer, "It's been fun. Look man, this is the beauty of...uh...'don't expect anything and just let the world come to you' and you can sometimes be pleasantly surprised." All the comics knew and felt comfortable with James, and he always killed. One of my best friends and best hosts in the entire country, he made every show better. Initially, I had asked my sister, Deanna, if James could stay with us for three weeks. That turned into three out of four weeks each month for nearly a year, until New York comedy opened back up in April of 2021, but I digress.

Back to the Big Jay show. Zac Amico featured, and Kunal Arora was granted a guest spot. Stage time was scarce, another side effect of the pandemic, but Jay was more than happy to give a spot to Kunal. During the show, the stepdaughter of a regular patron, a woman who had bought the VIP *SummerFest* Pass to every show, started drunkenly heckling and shouting out while the comedians were performing.

At one point, Luis was on stage talking about the ongoing LOS presidential election. (Luis, Big Jay, and Dave Smith from the *Legion of Skanks*, along with Ari Shaffir were running a bit to determine who was best to lead this group of unruly comics). The girl yells out "Fuck this place! Fuck Trump! Everyone's racist!". Luis wasn't talking about Democrats or Republicans. He was talking about comedians! Most comedians don't discuss politics, unless they have a specific following. This lovely gal had been a distraction the entire show. Working comedians are familiar with this type of behavior and know how to deal with it, usually in a funny way. Big Jay is no exception. I told him, while Luis was still on stage, that I wanted to remove her. He maintained that he needed her and would let me know if it becomes a problem. Jay is a master of crowd work, so I had no worries.

Jay was doing his thing, killer crowd work, including interacting with this girl. He had been talking to and about her for five minutes, at least, until she finally realized and barely coherent slurred, 'Who me?" That's the kind of self-awareness she had. None. The family starts to escort the daughter out. The crowd starts going nuts and applauding. The brother had stayed behind. I start to walk with the mom and stepdaughter, to let everyone know I'm handling it. While we were walking out, there was a few minutes of uncalled-for-interaction from her brother towards Jay and the crowd. The brother goes to confront Big Jay, who's about a football field away from where I was. I started to run as fast as I could, but it wasn't fast enough. Before I know it, I'm witnessing him grab Jay by the ankle, pull him off his stool and onto the ground. It was Jerry Springeresque.

A video, that captures those split seconds, shows Jay getting grabbed and Luis, the self-proclaimed Puerto Rican Rattlesnake, who was behind Jay during all this, springing into action. Because the video is so grainy, it almost looks like Luis was the second attacker on the sandy knoll, but he was, in fact, lightning quick to defend his friend.

The fans started flocking to Jay, Luis, and the brother. Everyone's wrestling with this guy. This whole melee happened within about two minutes from when Jay was about to wrap up the show. Seeing what was happening, I ran over, like an NFL referee, just moving guys off the pile to get to the football. I got to the bottom of the mound to find out one of the patrons had pepper sprayed the dad and the brother. The dad got up and kept repeating 'Not again!' 'Not again!" All I could think was, THIS HAS HAPPENED BEFORE??

The police arrive, the brother gets arrested, and things get sorted out. Before anyone got home the news of the attack on Big Jay had spread to New York. Ari Shaffir posted the video of the attack on Instagram and Burt Kreischer shared it, commenting, "Comedy's back, baby!" That event, publicly, put us on the map. It went worldwide.

Everyone was talking about us. Joe Rogan showed the video, Barstool did a segment, and countless other media outlets picked up the story. I was bombarded with emails, texts, and calls. I got a particularly unexpected phone call from *Page Six* in New York. It came up from Bermuda on my caller id. The guy on the other end, asking me about the skirmish, had an English accent. I thought the guy was a fake and without hesitation responded, what was meant to be tongue in cheek, "I guess the guy was trying to defend his sister's honor, although if you met her, I'm not sure how much honor there was to defend."

The next day, while out jogging along the Perkiomen Trail near the Schuylkill River with my sister Deanna, James Mattern, and Kunal Aurora, I got a call from Jim Breuer's manager. He had heard good things from Jessica Kirson having been there a week earlier, Day 12, the night before

Yannis. We were deciding on the date that Jim would perform, and he interjected, "Hey, by the way, what happened at your place last night?" My eyes widened and my eyebrows went straight up in the air. That's when I knew everyone had heard what happened. I let them know we had security in place and would keep the comedians, as well as the audience, safe. I hung up the phone and gave the loudest, "Woo-hoo!" I could muster.

After the run, Kunal, sipping on his smoothie, encouragingly congratulated me. When we first started doing outdoor shows, Kunal recommended that I go after the biggest comics and names I could, since literally everyone was stuck at home during the pandemic. How right he was. Over Labor Day weekend, Sam Morril came to perform. Like a lot of other comedians, including myself, Sam had doubts about outdoor comedy shows. The acoustics alone gave us all pause. He agreed to come, mainly because Sam is constantly working out new jokes and, of course, at the time we were one of the only places in the world where that could happen.

It was a nice, warm night, and as Sam's on stage, fireworks started going off directly behind and above him, almost as if they were planned. Royersford, being densely populated, outlawed fireworks, so these were definitely rogue. We snapped a photo of Sam going over new material on his phone just as an explosion of light, seemingly generated from the top of the homemade stage, disrupts his set. He was not happy, because as soon as that one finished more fireworks started going off across the river in Spring City.

All that aside, Sam was fine, relieved actually. He had planned on hiring a videographer to record this set for a special he was doing about comedy during the pandemic. Had he paid to film it, he would have been really upset. I thought that we might have blown the chance to ever get Sam back, but gratefully, he saw the upside and ended up coming back in December, in between Christmas and New Year's.

The saying goes 'lightning never strikes the same place twice'. Well, for SoulJoel's it struck four times: Louis CK's surprise performances, the Big Jay incident, getting Dave Attell as the *SummerFest* finale, and booking Jim Breuer to multiple sold out shows. It was boom, boom, boom, boom, all within 30 days of doing outdoor comedy at the end of the summer of 2020. Now everyone wanted to come to SoulJoel's, whether it was to perform or see a show. The list of top-notch comedians who graced our sandy stage was unbelievable. Too many to name.

From January 1, 2020, to January 1, 2021, we arranged over 200 acts. Because of continued government restrictions, we weren't allowed to go back inside for 16 straight months. We continued to adapt and grow, making conditions for our artists and audiences better and better, even through circumstances that were beyond our control.

Chapter Four – No Train, No Gain

      Imagine the sun setting, relaxing in the sand with a buddy and a beer, surrounded by beautiful trees and a quiet river rolling by in the background, while your favorite comedian is on stage, three words away from their punchline. Suddenly the rumbling of a 20-car freight train comes thundering by, drowning out the capper and, at first, befuddling the comic. That's what doing outdoor shows next to a train track, where trains ran all day long, every day, was like.

      There was no set schedule for these freight trains, none listed publicly, at least. It seemed nearly impossible to overcome, but it became part of the shows, thanks to some very quick, flexible comedians and an understanding, easy-going audience. I remember Mike Cannon quickly adjusting to the times, admitting that before the pandemic a loud waiter or waitress interrupting a show would upset him. But now, during the pandemic, he was doing all new material, as was the case with most comics, and figured he'd take a break and let the train ramble by for five minutes.

Jim Breuer came back for his second time, in April of 2021. As soon as he heard the train, in true Breuer fashion, he reacted and the whole place went nuts.

The night after the Big Jay Incident, Chuck Nice was the scheduled headliner. With the chaos of the night before, we were expecting, and half hoping for, a regular, run-of-the-mill, great comedy show. Instead, we got a run-of-the-train, epic show. Chuck had performed at SoulJoel's before, but this was his first time outside, in the sandlot. As the whistle got louder, and the train slowly approached the stage area, Chuck ran down the steps and started chasing it up the hill. It was the first and only time a comedian chased down a train. It was obvious to all that Chuck hadn't planned this, how could he?

At this point our outdoor shows were barely a month in, so unless he spoke to one of the other comics, there was no way he knew about the freight train intrusion. He made it seem like he was mad at the train for not only interrupting his set, but not even considering taking a detour! It certainly was a night, well, all together, a weekend to remember.

To this day, audience members bring up that Chuck Nice show, telling me they miss the loud interruption of the roaring locomotive because of the spontaneous bits that followed. It's been suggested, more than once, that I play an unexpected train sound over the speakers during a show...by the patrons, of course, not the comics.

As famous as our stage backdrop is now, there was none in the beginning. We built a 2x4 pagoda-like structure on the truck bed for the performers, hung some ferns, or as Bobby Kelly called them 'succulents', and had a couple of spotlights.

Local businesses started contacting me wanting to sponsor SoulJoel's. We started hanging a variety of banners from neighboring establishments, a quilt of logos, which quickly became fodder for almost every show. The best part was we didn't solicit any of them, all of the businesses reached out to us asking how they could support us by becoming a sponsor. Jim Breuer improvised a skit by sticking his head through an empty patch among the banners, acting like a train conductor giving a tour through Royersford. "Coming up on the left-hand side is SoulJoel's Comedy Club. They went outside during the pandemic and aren't sure when they're going back in." Jim had everyone dying when he riffed on the ReStore banner; a medical marijuana business, located on HIGH Street in POTtstown?! Some banners made it too easy!

Eventually, the backdrop filled in completely, displaying numerous ads from pizza shops to bladder control docs (that one, no joke, said, 'Laugh Don't Leak'). Comics would start off their sets by playfully busting on individual banners. Again and again, comics would zone in on one of the banners that featured two pretty lady realtors. As they got their shots off, I would shout from the back of the crowd, "That's my mom and sister!" and it actually was! For those who didn't know, comics and crowds alike, it came as a shock, making the observations awkward, then instantly hysterical, as they realized I wasn't offended. Occasionally, my mom and sister would be sitting in the audience, which made everyone howl with laughter. You gotta have thick skin in this business.

I did a fundraiser with Joe DeRosa and Dan Soder for my grandmother once, when she and my aunt worked for ARC. In the middle of playfully picking on my maw, Dan quips, "You know your grandson's high-strung?!" If you've ever been to a show at SoulJoel's, you've most undoubtedly heard a lot of jabs come my way. Don't worry, I love it as much as the audience does. Years later, Sam Tallent made his debut at SoulJoel's outside in the dome, spending most of time making fun of every single sign tied together as the backdrop. I had never seen Sam's stand-up prior to that night, so I didn't know what to expect. He didn't tell a single prepared joke for 45 minutes. From time to time, comedians will break the fourth wall to ask for a drink, bottle of water, or how long they've been on stage, but Sam kept calling to me. I'd answer or start to walk to the stage, and he'd act like that wasn't what he really wanted and that I didn't understand sarcasm and if he really needed me, he would let me know. This ping-pong back and forth had the audience and I dying laughing.

A lot of comics start sets by commenting on local events or traffic, etc., warming up and ingratiating themselves with the fans. The banner (along with the train) humor went a step above. The crowd ate it up and, in turn, patronized the local businesses. Another win-win. I've thought about contacting someone from the Reading Railroad. It would be interesting to know if any of those conductors saw or knew what was going on.

Handling the unknown became a juggling act. I was comfortable and knowledgeable about being a comedy producer, promoting events, cultivating audiences, and working with comedians. SoulJoel's had tackled the outdoors, audiences, and entertainers. Gears were grinding cooperatively. The global pandemic, however, tossed a couple of wrenches into that well-oiled machine that, thus far, I hadn't had to deal with on such a large scale. We were the biggest game in town, as far as public gatherings, at a time when a group of more than ten was taboo. Now I was dealing with a hovering health department, the police handling noise and large gathering complaints, and the government's perpetual adjustments to rules and restrictions. One thing I knew was that I couldn't give up, no matter the cost. I could feel we were making history. I didn't know to what degree, but I knew it felt right because we weren't hurting anyone or breaking any laws.

We have been blessed with the best audiences in the world. I've met a lot of wonderful, funny people and made some very good friends. But there isn't a bushel of apples without a worm or two. Our outdoor shows covered 10 to 15 hours a week, tops, but some people found it their business to complain. We complied with the borough's noise ordinance, barring one time when we went over, having left the music on after a show. People would drive by in their cars and gawk, like we were caged animals at a zoo. We weren't on a through street, so you had to intentionally turn into our cul-de-sac.

The first time Pete Dominick was booked, he saw some nosey onlookers and quipped, "SoulJoel is the best comedy promoter. You have me believing these people are here checking the place out for next week's show?" After we made national news, that is just what happened. People started finding out about us and would come from near and far, just to check us out. Not always with good intentions.

One incident happened prior to one of Breuer's shows. A guy on a Harley rode up and started taking pictures. Instantly, I began walking up the hill toward him. I was a former wrestler in high school and college, and I walk like one. However, I had just recently decided to wear pink every Sunday, mimicking Tiger Woods's style of wearing red for every championship. On a much smaller scale, obviously.

As it was Sunday, not only was I head to toe in pink; pink hat, pink shirt, pink shorts, Joey St. John was working topless alongside me. I guess a guy's gotta even out his tan. As I reached the biker, he bellows, "You the owner?" I nodded yes. "It's time to turn down your comedians, I'm trying to raise my family." "Hey buddy, I'm trying to raise my family, too, and survive this pandemic. We're in compliance and shut down when we're supposed to." He comes back with, "All I hear is filthy language." I knew this wasn't probable, because our speakers were pointed towards the river, which was directly beyond the lot. I had already tested our sound out by going across the Schuylkill River and knew what you could hear was muffled. After calmly confronting him with facts, he rode off, never to be heard from again.

About a month later, with a packed audience, Dan Soder was headlining for the first time. Mayor Jenna of Royersford contacted me with a complaint after his show. A resident grumbled about the noise and bad language. Come to find out this specific bellyacher lived behind the stage, in the opposite direction of the speakers, with a very active railroad in between. Because she lived behind the stage, it was even less likely that she or anyone else could decipher the words, let alone hear the show at all. Not to mention, these residents decided to live in a neighborhood within a stone's throw of a 24/7 freight train, but it's an outdoor comedy show that sends them over the edge to complain to their local government.

We were trying to keep comedians working, feeling good about themselves, while also providing quality entertainment for thousands of people trying to feel normal and have a laugh, during one of the darkest times in our country's history.

Another unwelcome disturbance came when a local senator attended a show. She never introduced herself. I only found out she was there because of the attention she caught from the comic on stage. Comics tend to focus on the one person not enjoying themselves, in a crowd of those who are.

The senator was scrolling on her phone, while Raanan Hershberg was on stage, during a fundraiser. He started in on the lady, "Yep, I got into comedy to be ignored. I will not stop talking until you start paying attention. What? Did you decide to support the cause and do your taxes during the show?" and went on a five- or so-minute rant, until the lady finally picked up her head. At that exact moment, behind the stage, a car started, which made it even funnier.

What was hard to comprehend was that this was the same senator forwarding all of the complaints from the health department. Never once did she come down to introduce herself when we were inside or outside in Royersford. Inside, it was a short time, but for those 16 months outside, we were the fastest growing business in town. It was hard to understand why she hadn't come by to introduce herself and see the place, firsthand. Now, given the opportunity, instead of genuinely experiencing what we had to offer, she decided to sit on her phone, distracting the audience and the comic during a fundraiser. A complete sign of disrespect. Next time, just stay home and write a check. But that's politics, right? You must show face at events. Or do you?

Fortunately, the bumps we encountered were minor irritants. Overall, SoulJoel's was moving along nicely. For almost a year and a half, we were outside doing shows, hosting 55,000 people from 27 different states, all while following guidelines set by the CDC during the pandemic. Thousands of people brought in by SoulJoel's directly and positively impacted the local economy. Droves of comedy fans patronized local businesses including restaurants, hotels, and shopping at the stores.

Royersford, a borough, not even a town, that has less than 5,000 full-time residents, became the comedy capital of the world, from 2020 to 2021.

The club got another nice pop after Nikki Glaser headlined, one year after I first met her. James Mattern, Shuli, and I were leaving a gig in Vermont, heading to the next in Maine. As we drove around, trying to figure out where to grab a bite before heading out, in a city we'd never been to before, we spotted some familiar faces. On a fluke, I had suggested turning left down an unknown street. James spots Andrew Collin and Ahri Findling, two comics that regularly open for Nikki. We all ended up having breakfast together, which led to an in with Nikki. We booked her, and she, of course, crushed her sold out shows.

Prior to Nikki working at the club, she introduced me to Mike Missanelli, a radio personality, who retired from hosting *The Fanatic* in Philadelphia on 97.5 and serving as a sports journalist for *The Philadelphia Inquirer*. He invited her on *The Fanatic* to promote her shows.

Fast forward to Spring of 2022. I got tickets to a Phillies vs Mets game, in Philadelphia, and took my 10-year-old nephew, Garrett. We met and sat beside my best friend growing up, Gary and his son, Jack. Our seats were great, behind home plate, but the Phillies were losing. They were down 2-1 in the 7th, and it being a school night, my friend decided to take off. My nephew did not want to budge. He had a baseball and was determined it was getting signed by a player. All I could think, was, man, that rarely happens, but he is pretty headstrong.

In the meantime, he sees the Philly Phanatic and remembering what his grandma advised, "If you're at the game, you gotta meet the Phanatic!" ran over to meet him. I turned around to check on him and I spotted Mike. "Mike, I don't know if you remember me, but you came to my comedy club over the pandemic." I wasn't wearing a SoulJoel shirt or hat, but he remembered me. It made me feel good.

The Phillies ended up winning 3-2. Impressively, my nephew got his ball signed by the catcher, JT Realmuto, who had hit the game winning homerun. Dead set on getting that ball signed, Garrett had hung around the dugout until he got what he wanted. He did not lay down. He did not give up. He stuck to his dream and made it happen. Manifestation at its best. I feel like my team at SoulJoel's and I did the same throughout the pandemic, keeping comedy alive and building the dream. But we weren't done yet.

During the summer and fall of 2020, SoulJoel's amphitheater went through many forms. We started out with a temporary wooden platform in the middle of a dirt lot, quickly upgrading to a truck bed and tons of sand. We added a makeshift stage with a wall of canvas ads. We were adapting as we grew, always intent on building this club into something spectacular. Throughout our metamorphosis, our audiences and performers endured rain, heat, humidity, and chilly nights. With winter approaching and no relief in sight from the rigid government guidelines barring indoor gatherings, I knew I had to figure out a way to keep up this forward momentum.

Enter the dome.

Not Funny – The Soul Behind Joel

Chapter Five – Family

A brief intermission.

Family doesn't mean just blood relatives to me. I've been blessed with amazing people in my life, some I share DNA with and some I don't, but they are family either way.

In 2009, when I initially left my day job, my family was very worried. I had decided to cash out my 401k, quit my job, and pursue comedy fulltime, giving myself one year to live off that money. Why worry?? Looking back, cashing out my 401k a year after the market tanked probably wasn't the smartest move, but I figured my future was in applesauce at a retirement home either way, so, hey, why not? Besides, I was 29, not married, no kids, so as far as personally, the time for me was now.

Comedy was going well, but comedy doesn't pay a lot, especially in the beginning. Remember, I did a show where I made no money, just trying to gain experience and a following. At times, it was overwhelming, I felt like my dream was in reach, but I needed help. I did not want to go back and get a nine to five. Luckily, my mom loaned me money twice. For years, she had been putting money aside for my wedding. But my life, my lover, my lady is comedy, so I asked if I could borrow that money. Turns out 15 years later, I'm still not married, but I did pay her back. Maybe that little nest egg will be used for tuxes and table settings one day, but for now comedy's a fine girl.

Two of my biggest supporters were my dad's mom, who I called Maw, and my mom's dad, Pappy. As doting grandparents, they loved that their grandson was pursuing his dreams and supported me anyway they could. I was on the schedule for quarterly shows at the State Theater in Uniontown for the last three or four years my grandmother was alive. Recruiting local charities to sell tickets, I would split the money raised in half and donate half back to them. My grandmother, full white head of hair and all, would drive around dropping off tickets to be sold and collecting money from ones that were. She was my local muscle and original street team.

In the months leading up to the event, I would have the tickets mailed directly to her and she would organize everything. The night of the shows, while collecting the tickets right before curtain call, I would feel a gentle nudge to my side. This sweet, sweet lady, in charming grandma fashion whispers, "So how did we do?" Which always cracked me up, because no matter the answer she never intended to get paid. It was never about the money - she was supporting me.

Some family members show support in other ways, like my 92-year-old grandfather. Yannis Pappas and I were performing in Pittsburgh in front of 12 people, six of whom were related to me on my mother's side, including my grandfather. While wearing a 'World's #1 Grandfather' shirt, he gets up on stage, grabs the microphone out of Yannis' hand and starts telling jokes. I was very embarrassed. Yannis still brings it up, often roasting me while on stage. My grandfather's unconventional support was out of love and fun and I knew that, I just wish it had been in more of a sit-down-and-clap kind of way.

Seriously though, I appreciate all the support I received over the years. They would all come to my shows, and not just the bringer shows. Firsthand, they got to see how much laughter I brought and the effect I had on a crowd. People would approach my mom, dad, and stepdad, gushing about how much they enjoyed the show. One person even shared, with my mom, that this had been the first time they had left their house since losing their spouse. It meant a great deal to all of us.

My very first attempt at opening a comedy club was with my sister Deanna and our brother-in-law, Scott Ready, who's married to our youngest sister, Laura. Deanna, as I mentioned before, helped SoulJoel's grow to its current state with her ideas, organizational skills, and hard work. Together, the three of us pitched our business plan to a place in Mount Holly, New Jersey, with the idea of calling it Iron Works. The name came from The Battle of Iron Works, a series of skirmishes that took place during the American Revolution, near Mount Holly. After we laid out our plans with the town council, we waited. And waited. We never heard back from them directly but found out they went with another outlet and used our business plan. Like John Paul Jones declared, "I have not yet begun to fight!". On my seventh endeavor, I opened SoulJoel's in Royersford. Deanna was, and still is, a realtor. Scott was, and still is, an executive chef. Both had families to take care of, but still they found time to help me, no questions asked.

Towards the end of my run at the Valley Forge Casino, I met Jay Ciccarone, by coincidence. He'd shown up for a show but had accidentally bought tickets for a different night. That serendipitous encounter led to him and I talking and quickly becoming friends. Eventually, when I would leave the Royersford location to move to

SunnyBrook, Jay was an instrumental part of me securing an SBA loan, by helping me land a lender. I solicited advice from him, almost every day, trying to figure out where I was going to relocate during that hectic, stressful time. I was a friend in need, and he was a friend indeed.

What would you say if I told you Dave Matthews came to shows every week, when we were inside at the Royersford location? In fact, he came out of nowhere and offered to build our stage. Dave, a guy who looks more like Larry the Cable Guy than the singer (gotcha) really took pride in helping me build something from scratch. It's guys like Dave who really helped piece SoulJoel's together.

Scott Chamberlin is another person I consider family. We started SoulJoel Productions together. It's funny, I would introduce him as my partner, which would raise a few eyebrows, because we were roommates and neither of us were married, at the time. I would always have to clarify. Scott helped lay the foundation for building relationships with a lot of comedians. Through many hours and late nights, he was another integral part of growing SoulJoel's to what it is today.

My stepdad, Joe Lawrence, who's been dating my mom for over half my life, is a retired police officer and a great man. Ever since the Big Jay incident, he has been on hand, with my best friend Gary Carty, to head up our security efforts for all the big shows. One day, Deanna asked Joe if (I) could book any comedian who would it be? His answer, and I'll never forget it, was Andrew Dice Clay. Spoiler alert: His wish came true.

My aunt and grandmother almost killed James Mattern. You can tell how good a friend you got, when even after an almost accidental death, they stick around. I've mentioned James throughout this book, but I would be remiss if I didn't include my brother-from-another-mother in the family chapter.

James and I had gone to my dad's hometown to do a fundraiser for the fire department, where my cousin, Paul Richardson, was a member. After the show, my grandma handed us some brownies that my Aunt Amy had made. Of course, I start popping them like Tic Tacs, and James starts in on his. After one bite, he asks, "Is there peanut butter in this?" "There sure is!" Grandma answers. "Well, I'm allergic to peanuts." He exclaims and lapses into kaleidoscope vision. Luckily, we were able to quickly get him into a nearby ambulance and he spent the night at the hospital. The next day, on our drive back to New York, to make conversation, I casually remark, "Last night was great, huh?" "Well, I almost died." James returns. "Yeah, but it was a hot crowd and we got paid to do comedy on the road." "I spent the night in the hospital, and you got that hotel room for no reason." A friend to the end, thank God that night wasn't it.

Not Funny – The Soul Behind Joel

From NY beginnings to PA present

Our wall of fame

The late, great Gilbert Gottfried

Closing the dome in Royersford with Moorestown Alumni

Not Funny – The Soul Behind Joel

Joel as Cuppy at the Broad Street Run in 2016

Joel's mom and stepdad in front of his photo on the wall of fame - Collegeville Italian Bakery Pizzeria Napoletana

Joel Richardson and Lu

Joel and mom in front of SunnyBrook / Laura, mom, Deanna

Family Dinner

Deanna, Joel, Laura / Joel and his dad

Not Funny – The Soul Behind Joel

Yannis Pappas and Joel

Joel Richardson and Lu

Longtime SoulJoel headliner Jessica Kirson outside the dome with Lu and her daughter

Live taping of *Tuesdays with Stories!* with guests Shane Gillis and Sean Donnelly

Not Funny – The Soul Behind Joel

The many looks of Joel Richardson

Vic Henley, Joel and Judd Jones opening night at SoulJoel's in Royersford

Not Funny – The Soul Behind Joel

Pre-stage, pre-sand, pre-dome - July 2020

Greg Stone and the rant that built the stage

Gill Moyer (not pictured) tried to make a carpenter out of Joel

The community of small businesses started to rally around SoulJoel's

Surprise drop-in Jim Norton

James Mattern feeling the magic

1st Annual Summerfest 2020

Sam Morril and a rogue firework

The Joey St. John

Joel Richardson and Lu

1st Ruddy and Dean's with Moorestown Alumni - Gaetano Barbuto, Gary Carty, and Ryan Govito

Paul Virzi with Joel

Not Funny – The Soul Behind Joel

(L) Raanan Hershberg repping SoulJoel's at the Comedy Cellar in New York
(R) Fan Mimi repping SoulJoel's in California with Dave Attell and Louis Katz

(L) Lifelong fan Kris Scharf with headliner Dan Soder

(R) Joel's smallest fan, standing at 4' 9", Laura Lee

The Dome

Approx. 65' x 100' x 25', seating about 400

After shows outside the dome

(L) Robert Kelly and Joe Russell

(R) Mike Vecchione, Ari Shaffir, Mark Normand, and Lu

Comedian's favorite audience member and co-host of *The Bring 'Em Out!* podcast – Alan Hill

Can't ya just hear this pic?

Joel's stepdad, mom, Joel, stepbrother, and sister at the opening of SoulJoel's in Royersford

Joel and his mom at the Tri-County Young Professional Awards Gala in 2020

Not Funny – The Soul Behind Joel

Announcing Andrew Dice Clay performing at SoulJoel's on the sign The Collegeville Bakery – a supporter from day one

Joey St. John and Joel leaving Royersford – November 2021

Joel Richardson and Lu

Spotted Hill Farm longtime sponsor Donna and her friend Vicki

Not Funny – The Soul Behind Joel

Big Jay Oakerson, Lu, and Luis J. Gomez after "the Big Jay incident" heard round the world

Gary Carty, security for SoulJoel's since 2020

Kelly and BJ McElmurry, the first wedding held at SoulJoel's - December 2019

Joel's aunt, uncle and cousins at the 1st NYE at SunnyBrook with the singer of The Uptown Band Erich Cawalla

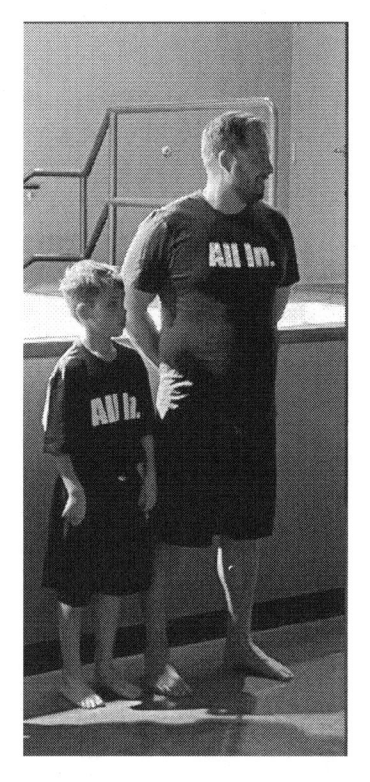

Joel's second baptism with his nephew who chose to be there without being asked

Joel Richardson and Lu

James Mattern and Joel at the outdoor pandemic Halloween show – October 2020

"SoulJoel's is the hottest club in town."
-Mark Normand

Sam Tripoli with Lu

Joel's grandfather asleep at one of Joel's shows

Joel Richardson and Lu

Chapter 6 – Welcome to the Thunder and Lightning, Snow, Rain, and Hurricane Dome.

Because COVID numbers had spiked, it wasn't possible for us to go back inside. The CDC declared the six-feet-apart rule and with our normal capacity of 150 at the time, it would have sliced our audience to about 25 to 30 people. I wouldn't have been able to pay for the comics, much less my rent or staff. Constantly having to adapt and cold temperatures quickly approaching, for a brief time, we set up a heated tent. Blow heaters were needed and bought, but they weren't cutting it. Eventually, we switched to tall patio heaters, which worked much better. I kept buying more and more of them, as they became available, until I accumulated about 35. It wasn't cheap. After purchasing the heaters, I also had to pay for weekly propane pickups and drop offs. At this point, I had no other option.

The first show in the heated tent featured Adam Ferrara. The following show had Dave Attell back for his second appearance. My landlord, at the time, would not let anyone in the building, not even to use the bathrooms. With the government shutting places down every day for the slightest infraction, I didn't blame him at all. The answer to nature's call was trucking in five porta-potties and that's what everyone used for the 16 months to follow. Dave lovingly referred to us as "the saddest farmer's market he had ever been to". Pros, as they are, these two veteran headliners endured the unique surroundings, and everyone had a ball.

We had killer, eclectic lineups. Sherrod Small came twice in the Fall, the second time was during Thanksgiving weekend with Sam Jay. One of the first times Joe List brought Louis CK, it had poured most of the day, so much so that the tent had flooded. We were scooping water out from inside the tent, until about an hour before that show.

Ed Bassmaster, who was extremely hot on the internet at the time, performed two shows in one night. If you're not familiar with him, he's created several characters, all with different personalities and completely different outfits. Even to this day, he reminds me how bad it was having a small side tent as a changing room. He performed five different characters during an hour-and-a-half show, twice in one night. Michelle Wolf crushed her two shows with Cipha Sounds and, of course, James Mattern hosting. Shane Gillis also headlined and killed the two shows he did in the tent. Mike Vecchione came back and was shocked and delighted to see all the changes we had made since he first headlined, back on that rainy day in July. It wasn't quite the dome, yet, but it was a covered, heated space, at least.

The Wednesday before Thanksgiving of 2020, exactly three years to the day, as these words are being typed, Jimmy Shubert was scheduled to perform. Jimmy is a great friend and mentor to me. Not only has he recommended countless comedians to SoulJoel's but is a Comedy Store legend and still one of the best touring comedians. As people were walking down the hill, and I was checking them in on my phone, everyone's phones started buzzing. An alert had been issued, basically warning people not to gather or go out in public unless absolutely necessary. Thanksgiving Eve is historically the biggest party night of the year. There were so many blocks stacked against us.

Judy Gold ended up being our last show in the heated tent. The dome was coming, but it was late. The crew that came to assemble the dome were a couple of guys from Kentucky, who looked like they were on meth. Instead of the promised four-day turnaround, it took them 18.

Unfortunately, the original tent was a rental and had been picked up by the rental company. Tents were a hot commodity because of COVID restrictions and were very expensive due to high demand. We had shows planned for inside the dome that ended up happening outside, with no cover. We had no choice but to hold the performances in the lot, next to where the dome was being built, outside in the elements. To this day, I've never stiffed a comedian. When we book talent, a deal is a deal. The shows must go on.

Between Christmas and New Year's, we had booked a monster lineup. A lot of big acts have riders or a list of demands for the venue where they will perform. Sometimes it's as simple as a specific canned cola or a bowl full of brown only M&Ms. Not one of the acts scheduled put 'must have a roof' on their rider, so I was in the clear! I joke, of course, but you have to, or you just feel defeated and start to think why bother?

The first show, that should have been under the dome, was H. Foley and Kevin Ryan, the *Are You Garbage?* guys. Then came Darrell Hammond of *Saturday Night Live*. Next to follow was a meet and greet with Santa Claus. Yeah, we got the big guy. Then came Mark Normand, Sam Morril, Joe Machi, Derek Gaines and Jeremiah Watkins. To welcome in the New Year, Andy Fiori and Sean Donnelly hosted a double headliner show. Chris Distefano became a part of the open-air club, as did

Eleanor Kerrigan. Eleanor's show turned out to be particularly significant.

At this point, any profits made from the previous summer were dwindling. There were so many unforeseen added costs, we were teetering on the edge of dipping into the red. Because the shows that came between the tent and dome were outside, the weather was magnified. It was cold and miserable, so they didn't always pack out. I lost money on every single one of those shows.

Eleanor approached me after her show and asked if I would be ok if she gave my phone number to Andrew Dice Clay. Andrew. Dice. Clay. "Absolutely." I responded. I had had opportunities to ask Eleanor for Dice's info., but I never did. I never brought it up. A lot of club owners and bookers would use her to get to him, but I learned a lesson early on. Julian McCullough taught me to treat comedy like the mafia: keep your mouth shut and you'll be ok. Besides, Eleanor was incredible on her own merit, killing every time she stepped on stage. Although I was excited at the thought of her giving Dice my number, I actually forgot about it. I was so busy with the dome, the ongoing restrictions, booking acts, negotiating with managers and agents, locking in hotel room dates, promoting the club, all while operating with a paper-thin staff. I was barely keeping my head or my finances above water, but I never once shorted any of the talent.

Finally, the dome construction was finished, so we moved the heaters in and set up shop. Aunt Mary Pat, coincidentally, ended up being our first show under the dome, as she was when we opened inside.

Unexpectedly, I got a call on January 8th from Beverly Hills. Fully expecting to be asked about my car's extended warranty, I answered, and it was Dice. Right away he asks, "Did Eleanor tell you I was gonna call or is this a surprise?" As I previously mentioned, Eleanor had told me, but up till then I had blocked it out of my mind, thinking I'll believe it if it ever happens. It happened and the next thing I know, we're negotiating dates and money.

Days before that conversation, I had been on the phone with Jim Breuer's agent, setting up some dates for his second appearance in April. It just so happens that Jim's agent is also Dice's. I had previously asked him about booking Dice, and he had explained that Dice, being somewhat of a germaphobe, was not traveling. Prior to the shutdowns, to book an act, I mainly dealt with comedians directly. It was rare that I booked through agents and managers. This personal perk of the pandemic got Andrew Dice Clay to come to SoulJoel's. Practically every conversation I had with him seemed like he was testing me. After 40 plus years in the business, he rarely had to deal with a new booker/comedy club owner, much less directly. Honestly, I'm pretty sure most of it was for his own enjoyment.

I made every demand. I booked the right hotel. I ensured the best local limousine company. "Little boy blew. OHHHHH! He needed the money." Thank God it all worked out. Those three shows, plus the two nights Chris Distefano did over Martin Luther King Jr. weekend, brought us out of the red and into the black. Smooth sailing from here on out. Ha!

Wednesday night, I get a phone call from Tim Dillon's agent. This can't be good. Tim was coming in from Austin to do four sold out shows. His agent explained to me that there had been a freak ice storm. It was all over the news. Every nearby airport, including Austin, Dallas, San Antonio and Houston, were booked solid and overwhelmed, if not shut down completely. An ice storm in Austin, Texas. You can't make this shit up. We were forced to cancel the weekend. One step forward, two steps back.

Our calendar was pretty full already, so I scrambled to reschedule Tim's shows. I desperately needed those shows and decided to do something I had never done before: move an already booked act. It was such a hard decision for me. I am a loyal guy. In the middle of this turmoil, Dice sensed that I was more wound-up than usual. We talked about my dilemma and, I will never forget this till the day

I die, Dice made it clear, strictly businesslike, that I had to move the already booked show. As hesitant as I was, I was up against a wall. It was a survival tactic, a business decision, never personal. I agreed and scheduled Tim for the first weekend in March. Sometimes, challenges come as surprised blessings. Tim's original four-sold-out-shows turned into six sold out shows. One step back, two steps forward.

Two weeks before Tim Dillon's weekend, were Dice's shows. I woke up Thursday morning, the third and final day of this run, to snowfall. Dice, being on LA time, was still asleep. Now my mind was racing. I had paid Dice in advance and worried that I would have to cancel tonight's performance and issue refunds to the ticket holders. When he finally woke up, we discussed options. His answer was an obscure quote from a movie. He told me to ask him if he was ready for tonight. I obliged, "Are you ready for tonight? "You don't see me backing down, do ya?" he delivered. Due to the stress I was under, I didn't exactly laugh. I was never able to verify that as a direct quote from a movie. Dice took the stage under the dome, like a champ, looking like a snow globe with flurries swirling around him. We went on a tear from there.

Russell Peters, arguably one of the biggest international comics around came after Tim, who, by the way, cost us an RV rental, sort of. Tim had been caught by my landlord, Rick Lewis, smoking a cigarette inside with the door open, filling the lobby area and our green room with smoke. Rick subsequently locked us out of the building for any future gigs. Again, I don't blame him, he was trying to abide by the rules. We ended up having to rent an RV for Russell. Another unexpected cost. But it was March, and March weather is still chilly, especially at night. It kinda felt like a movie set. Russell's on stage, riffing with the crowd and points to one of the banners. "What's Lewis Environmental?" (We had given Rick a banner at no cost for initially helping with the sand and other accommodations.) "Your landlord? The one who locked you out of the building?!" The entire crowd of the sold-out show howled, as did I. The next killer to come to SoulJoel's was D.L. Hugley. I had only dreamed of ever working with him, and now he was coming for four shows in Royersford, PA.

As hungry and eager as most comedians were for stage time at SoulJoel's, not every comedian was grateful. I still remember, it was Memorial Day weekend 2021 and we had booked Earthquake. He was one of a few comedians that were randomly scheduled to perform on their birthdays without us knowing: him, Ms. Pat, and Jimmy Schubert.

Friday night, he pulls up in his car and his manager pulls up in another. Now we had booked his shows five months prior, when the shutdown mandates were still in place. Although still in the middle of the pandemic, restrictions were easing up, and we were still utilizing the dome. Even New York didn't fully open back up for indoor shows until April of 2021. It was a tough time to navigate.

It was a rainy miserable weekend, he had just done an indoor show in Harrisburg, it was his first time at SoulJoel's, and now he had to do a show outside on a fake beach on his birthday. I get it, those conditions might shake up a person's mood, but he had agreed to this date and venue. There are always two sides to a story, but his side was packing heat.

His manager comes walking down the hill with a visible gun in his waistband, already intimidating, but trying to claim that we tricked his client into doing an outdoor show. To this day, if you look up SoulJoel's on Google, you'd more than likely see images of the outdoor comedy dome. We had sold a lot of tickets for both shows that weekend, we started to panic a little. Here's a guy trying to strong-arm his way out of a commitment, and here we were left to figure out what to do next.

Eventually, his opener talked to Earthquake, telling him that people had driven as far as western Pennsylvania and Virginia Beach, even booking hotel rooms to attend the show. He agreed to go on Friday, with no intention of doing the Saturday gig. Fortunately, he ended up fulfilling his commitment for all four shows. Everything turned out fine, but in the craziness of running around, scrambling back and forth trying to plug all the metaphoric leaks, my phone jumped out of my pocket and into a puddle, and I had to get a new one. But, lesson learned, make sure you always get a contract.

The dome, being a huge, white temporary structure that popped up during the pandemic, led a few passersby to think it was a vaccination clinic, which I always found funny. For the majority of fans, comics, staff, and myself, it became a symbol of hope. We kept comedy alive at a time when the country needed laughter, relief, and something to look forward to. People needed a pleasant distraction from the world's chaotic state. I was often told that just driving by, seeing the dome, would bring smiles to the faces of many. We kept comics working. I would hear comedians praising SoulJoel's on various media outlets and directly from the comics themselves. I still do. The comedy dome has forever positively branded us with providing entertainment through outdoor comedy shows during an unprecedented, remarkably dark period in the history of the world.

Chapter 7 – Leaving Rofo

Funny as it was, we couldn't let people continue to think the dome was a vaccination clinic. I hired my sign guys, CJ Santangelo and his partner Rob Lagassie, to stamp the side of the canvas dome with an 11 x 33 footprint of our logo. I met CJ and Rob after hosting a fundraiser for a local child dealing with cancer. These are the guys who made the yard signs for *Summerfest*, detailed the SoulJoel mobile, and all the background banners for our sponsors.

As they were attempting to place the sign, their truck got stuck. In retrospect, again, I have to think everything happens for a reason. The maintenance man for the property came out and ordered us to take the sign off the dome until I had permission from the borough. Apparently, a sign could be no bigger than 10 x 4 feet on a permanent structure. The key word there is permanent, because my permit for the comedy dome was for a temporary structure. I ended up arguing back and forth with one of the council members on social media. The president, seeing this, calls my sister Deanna, and asks her to make me stop. Me, not the member of his council arguing back. Her immediate response was, "Yeah, I'll have him stop, his time is better spent focusing on a permanent home for SoulJoel's, and it's not going to be Royersford." Everything came to a head. They were focused on running me out of town.

Without hesitation, they voted to revoke my permit for the dome, stating that it was for the use of a temporary structure and because restrictions were being lifted, it was no longer necessary. Did they think I would have spent $60,000 on a structure to be built granted on a temporary permit that could be lifted at any time? I had to hire a lawyer to fight them on their convoluted specifications. Normally, very few, if any, locals attend these council meetings, but because I was making a stir, they were forced to move the meeting outside to a park and call the police to take care of crowd control, if need be. It was so frustrating, and after complying with the town's rules thus far, I was ready to move on.

To this day, I have never seen the permit. Initially I was told to have the dome torn down by

August 6, 2021, less than two months away. The problem was twofold: I had acts booked out far past this date and the dome was as concrete a temporary structure as you can imagine. It would take three or four days to disassemble it and August 6th was a scheduled-out Friday. Thankfully, I was granted a reprieve, until the end of October.

During this whole time, rumors started flying, which our team would hear in person and on social media. One of the narratives I found most entertaining was gossip about me packing up and leaving Royersford to move back to New Jersey. For anyone keeping score at home, I had sold my house in New Jersey and moved into my sister's basement. Why would I move back all these years later? Life had pulled me further west. I wasn't about to become a salmon and force myself to swim against the stream and, ultimately, fate.

To some extent, the magic felt like it had been zapped from the air, but it didn't stop some cool things from happening. Kevin Nealon, *SNL* alumni known for several movies and the TV series *Weeds*, came for some extraordinary shows under the dome, along with The Rusted Root Duo. Both had reached out to us wanting to perform at the legendary dome. Rusted Root had reached out to my cousins, asking if they thought I'd have an interest in them playing at SoulJoel's. Musicians were beginning to hear about us, word was spreading throughout the country. Presto chango, I was feeling good again.

    The weekend that Kevin Nealon came to SoulJoel's started off by us booking him Thursday night at Rivers Casino, then two shows Friday and two on Saturday under the dome for the second annual *Summerfest* in August of 2021. I had met Kevin through Jay Black, one of the last comedians to headline SoulJoel's the week before the shutdown. Jay hyped us up, telling Kevin how amazing we were and how he must perform there. We ended up arranging the three-day weekend, and I met him that Thursday in the green room at Rivers Casino. I mentioned that Buddy Harris and Brendan Donegan were his openers.

    In addition to fulfilling any rider requirements, I have to navigate other considerations, too. Kevin requested that the comedians before him be clean. He's not a dirty comic, although he toes the line with some dark comedy, and wanted to save that for himself, which is reasonable and understandable. As we were leaving the green room, he wanted to check out the showroom and get a feel for the crowd, which a lot of comedians do. As we turn the corner, Brendan is walking towards us and Kevin promptly hits him with "Oh, are you Buddy or are you Brendan?" This astonished me, he had cared enough to remember both names of openers he's never met before and would most likely never see again. It spoke volumes about Kevin's character. Brendan responded who he was, and that Buddy was on stage now.

Buddy's in the middle of a joke as we walk into the back of the showroom. The first thing we hear is "...so this guy is sucking my dick...". (Side note: I forgot to remind Buddy that all of Kevin's openers have to work clean. So technically, this one is on me. Whoopsie cakes!) Kevin's eyebrows shot to the ceiling, and I practically had a panic attack. Not a great start, and now Kevin's the one with a bad taste in his mouth.

The next night we switched things up, as we had planned, with Brendan now hosting, leaving Buddy to feature. Kevin perks up and dryly jokes, "This is great fellas, am I hosting tomorrow night? Are you gonna do that bit about the guy sucking your dick again, because that was great." He sarcastically used the power of laughter to make his point, basically conveying 'ok you did it last night, but you better not do it tonight'. All in all, it ended up being a fantastic weekend.

The last show under the dome in Royersford, PA, was with the one and only Gilbert Gottfried. Towards the end of his show, I looked up at the sky and noted, to my best friend, Gary, who had served as head of security ever since the Big Jay ruckus, that I didn't think it was supposed to rain. He cracks, "Well it's raining, bub." As people filed out and headed to their cars, the dome started flooding. It didn't affect us, this time, but felt like a symbolic moment. The iconic dome was leaving Royersford, the way it came in, messy.

But how was I going to take this dome down? I had no one. Dave Matthews, luckily, came through by getting me in contact with a man named Scott Reese, a man I have saved in my contacts as 'Scott Angel'. Within days, Scott and his crew had disassembled and taken down the dome. My landlord had graciously extended our lease one week so that we could have the porta potties, the dome, and all our belongings removed from the property.

It was a mad couple of months trying to find a new location. Finally, in mid-October I settled on the temporary home of Westover Golf Course, owned by Vince Piazza brother of former Mets and Major League Hall of Famer, Mike Piazza. Anything to keep SoulJoel's going. Twenty minutes away from Royersford, it worked out perfectly for us and them, because the golf course was of little use over the winter.

Two weeks before our first show at Westover, with Andrew Dice Clay headlining, I was worried we didn't have enough time or staff to help sell tickets. I started talking strategy with my right-hand man, Joey St. John. Unanticipated, he informed me that he was leaving to pursue his dream of expanding his videography and photography business. It was his time. He was in his early thirties and had watched and helped me achieve my dreams. Although the timing was not ideal for me, I supported his decision. It was bittersweet. SoulJoel's was in the middle of yet another seemingly no-end-in-sight transition, but I was proud of him.

Soul-diering on, I never took my foot off the gas. Sal Vulcano from *Impractical Jokers* came with Chris Distefano, the first live show of their podcast, *Hey Babe!* People came from Arizona and California! SoulJoel's was nationwide. Drawing a crowd from the other side of the country, booking the biggest names in comedy was a 10-year plan, I never imagined it would happen in a year and a half. During the seven months at Westover, we also had Steve Byrne, Jeremiah Watkins and Steve Lee's live podcast *Scissor Bros*, Tommy Davidson, Judy Gold, and Tim Meadows.

However, the roller coaster ride I was on took a quick, stomach-turning dip. At the start of 2022, I went from three full-time employees to one. I had sold my home and moved in with my sister at the very beginning of this journey and part of that sale went to buy the dome. I was now forced to sell it, at a considerable loss. Live Nation, smelling my desperation, bought it for $25,000. The whole time, I'm still looking for a permanent location. I was unwilling to move back to New Jersey or even leave

Montgomery County. I had built up a fanbase and wanted to stay close. My options were dwindling.

After looking at what had to be 30 different venues and a blur of surrounding towns, nothing was sticking. I had fixed requirements, needing it to be accessible off Route 422, have ample parking, and space for outdoor comedy. The dome was a central part of SoulJoel's, and I felt it was imperative that it be resurrected. A couple of places looked promising, to the point that I hired architects and planners, but I would end up getting outbid or someone would swoop in with a cash offer.

At last, I announced that SoulJoel's was moving to Skippack, PA, twenty minutes north of Royersford. I made a video announcing the move and posted it on all the socials. Here we come. Screeeeech! Slam on the brakes. I had been working with a guy, behind the scenes, to secure this location. The town council of Skippack was excited about us taking over. Come to find out, my guy tells me that an unnamed gentleman from Royersford warned them not to let me open up there. What business was it of theirs?! This was beyond crazy. The deal at Skippack folded. I felt like a fraud having already made our move public.

Throughout this leg of my journey, there were a lot of setbacks. They never stopped me, but I felt them deeply. During all this, at one of my lowest points personally, I found a way to overcome and work through it. By writing and working my new material out on stage, I ended up with the best 15 to 20 minutes of my life. It was my tightest material, got the biggest laughs, and I was killing. But pain is where a lot of comedy comes from. Comedy is tragedy plus time, right? For me it certainly was, I had never been funnier.

Chapter 8 – SunnyBrook

SunnyBrook was it. I could feel it. Even the name evoked hope, and I was in desperate need of some. Back in my hometown of Moorestown, New Jersey, my very first job was at a swim club called Sunnybrook, and although completely unrelated to the SunnyBrook Ballroom in Pottstown, I took it as a sign.

While I was at my mom's house, still sulking over the Skippack deal falling apart, the phone rang and it's the realtor for SunnyBrook. Prior to Skippack failing, we were deciding between both properties. The realtor, Kevin, explained to my mom that the owner wanted to meet with me. Without hesitation I agreed, and we set up a meeting time for a few days later. Before heading to the introduction, I threw on my 'uniform', grey pants and signature SoulJoel t-shirt, that I normally would wear on stage. My sister, Deanna, looked at me up and down, and laughed, "Get in the car, you maniac." I had never worn SoulJoel's merch when looking for properties, I wanted to keep that information on the down low, but something made me pop on that shirt.

My mom was already at SunnyBrook, talking to their realtor, Kevin, and the owner, Chuck Galotti, as we arrived. I get out of the car, and Chuck squints as he reads my shirt. Surprised he declares, "I didn't know that you were the Joel that I was going to meet. I'm a big fan of your place! You wanna take over SunnyBrook?" He turns to his realtor, "You didn't tell me I was meeting with SoulJoel." Kevin was like, "I don't know who that is." They just assumed I was Joel Richarson, a guy looking to take over a wedding venue, not realizing my earlier experience with running a comedy club. I assured Chuck that any employee he had on staff would be offered a job and, if they choose to, would remain employees. Straight away, we started the process of me acquiring SunnyBrook.

Before you know it, we're agreeing on details and signing paperwork. Now was the time for Deanna and me to call our sister, Laura, and her husband, Scott, and persuade them to uproot their family and move to Pennsylvania. We needed Scott's expertise as a chef at SunnyBrook. He was the missing piece. He had more experience running a restaurant than I had in comedy, previously having been an executive chef in the Navy Yard with Bar Amis, now known as The Gatehouse, where he designed a seasonal menu every three months. Located near concert and sports stadiums in South Philly, he was used to feeding large crowds, especially as folks were grabbing a bite before the games or concerts. It's not easy for a restaurant to handle that kind of volume, all while giving the customer a great dining experience with exceptional and efficient service. Securing Scott would prove to be a great partnership as we obtained the SunnyBrook Ballroom, not only for the restaurant, but for catering weddings, proms, and banquets.

As they were milling over the idea of moving and figuring that all out, Deanna and I met with Chuck, the township manager, and the code officer of Lower Pottsgrove to seek approval for the dome to be raised from the dead. It was the best meeting I have had with a township, thus far. Things were looking good. Pottsgrove was looking forward to us coming to town and reviving historic SunnyBrook.

We were standing in a lobby of the former restaurant, Gatsby's, and a man I'd never seen before, a tall, light-skinned black man, who looked like Uncle Phil from *The Fresh Prince of Bel Air*, walked in and asked if Gatsby's was still a brewery. He divulged that he hadn't been in the area in over 10 years, drove to Pottsgrove from Delaware to drop someone off, and stopped by to check out the place. Additionally, he asks if we still had Ursula, the pipe organ and if George Batman still played it. Chuck Gulati informed him that, indeed Ursula was still going strong, as was George and as a matter of fact, he played her for the brunches they held on Mother's Day and Easter. The gentleman asks Chuck if he could take a look around. Chuck nods yes and they take off. Deanna and I mentioned that it was nice meeting him and told Chuck we'd see him later.

As we're standing there rehashing the meeting by our cars in the parking lot, Chuck comes sprinting out of the ballroom doors and calls to us, "You gotta get back in here! This guy's playing the organ!" Thinking back to this moment, the hair on the back of my neck stands up. The beautiful melody wafting from the pipes was from Beauty and The Beast, "Be our guest! Be our guest! Put our service to the test." I looked at this man and instantly thought of my mom's mom. She would have loved SunnyBrook. He even had flabby arms like her. (My grandmother thought "exercise was for horses"). As soon as he stopped playing, I told him about her and how she was a music teacher who played the organ every Sunday at church. He looks at me and noted, "That's what I do." Chills. As he gets up to leave, he adds, "I gotta head back to Delaware." Or Heaven, I thought. I drove home, pulled into the driveway, parked my car and sitting on the fence were two red cardinals. It was the first time that had happened to me and hasn't happened since. Positive signs were popping up everywhere.

Throughout my life I've been aware and encouraged by incidental evidence of signs or indications or signals or whatever you want to call them. They have helped guide me towards success, both personally and professionally.

When I was leaving Royersford, a man named Ed Nelson came into my life. I call him my spiritual advisor, but if you ask him, he would claim he's my spiritual brother. He and his now ex-wife started attending shows in the summer of 2021. The first show they attended was with headliner Rich Vos. If you know anything about Rich, you know he is a master of crowd work and maybe don't sit in the front row.

Rich is on stage working the crowd, sees Ed and his wife, and asks them where they are from. Neither answered and Rich jumped on the opportunity, "I don't blame you for not admitting where you're from in this tent full of white people." The area of Royersford is not a very mixed community, which was often noted by the comics, and Ed and his then wife are black. Just as Rich finishes his line, the Royersford police appeared in the back of the dome, which was not uncommon. If they were having a quiet night, they would stop by and check in on things and, honestly, enjoy a show while waiting for a call. Of course, Rich took full pro comic advantage of the situation looking over at me and scolding, "Great, Joel, the minute I started talking to the black guy, the cops show up." The whole crowd was in stitches.

About a month later, we had Bill Bellamy at the dome. Again, Ed Nelson and his wife showed up. "Do you remember me?" he asks. "Yeah, you're the couple from the Rich Vos show." I answered. We continued the conversation, and both realized we had a deeper connection. Ed started sending me countless messages, scriptures, and sermons that make even more sense in hindsight than they did originally. Through the many ups and downs, Ed's messages struck me and helped keep me level. To quote an especially meaningful one: "If God wants you to shine at 100 watts, shine at 100, don't shine at 60. God is using you to serve a purpose and there's nothing you can do to change that. This is God's work and His doing." I had never been more spiritual. Ed strengthened my belief in God, helping me see that there is a higher power and that everything happens for a reason. That being said, if it weren't for Rich Vos, I don't know how quickly I would have met Ed.

Vos will be performing at SoulJoel's March 22, 2024.

From there on, pieces started falling into place. Laura and Scott agreed to move to

Pennsylvania and put their house up for sale. In the meantime, they would move into Deanna's house, where I was also living. In total, Deanna, her four kids, me, Laura, Scott, their three kids, and their dog lived together for 10 months. Cousins were now growing up as siblings. We had the littles, the middles and the olders. It was tough, at times, as having that many people living together under one roof would be, but we made it work. In some ways, in effect, it became easier. Scott did all the grocery shopping and cooking, the kids always had someone to play with, plenty of adults to carpool, and there was always easy access to a babysitter. At long last, on October 31, 2022, I took over the SunnyBrook Ballroom, exactly three years after opening SoulJoel's on November 1, 2019, and one year after leaving Royersford on October 30, 2021. Too much to be coincidence, there was fate in those dates.

Shortly after taking over the SunnyBrook Ballroom, and I mean shortly, within an hour, the top two employees resigned from their positions. One of them called me from the parking lot and informed me they had dropped the keys on the desk and left. Never even meeting me face-to-face. The keys weren't labeled either, I had no idea what key went to what and, as luck would have it, there was a wedding previously booked for that night. The wedding, part of our contractual obligations, was one of the events scheduled that helped fill that first calendar year. We started weekly line dances on

Tuesdays, an open mic night, monthly swing, salsa, and bachata dances, and comedy shows Fridays and Saturdays, but we needed to really pack the calendar. And as it so happens, an unexpected cowboy intervention helped us do just that.

"Wherever a man dwells, he shall be sure to have a thorn-bush near his door." An old English proverb befitting the first few weeks at SunnyBrook. The night before Thanksgiving, conceivably the biggest drinking night of the year, I received a call from a good friend. He let me know that one of the bartenders was skimming the register. For example, a customer would order a round, the bartender would pour the drinks and charge the proper amount, for example, say $33.00. The patron would then hand them $40.00, which would, instead of being put into the register, be pocketed, while the $7.00 change was taken from the tip jar.

Cameras might be everywhere, catching things no one wants to see, but thankfully they caught what I needed to see that night. I was able to verify all parties involved and that what my friend warned me about was indeed true. When I confronted the employee, they doubled down and claimed to have put the money back in the register. My response was, "I have no problem watching the next four hours of this tape. We can get this up to a felony." Naturally, I had to fire this person, which led to me having to do something I had not done since college – bartend.

Before I took ownership of SunnyBrook, part of our agreement was they got the food and drink money, and I would take ticket sales from the events. The register systems were already programmed with predetermined prices set. When I started bartending, something I would never have done had I not had to fire that dishonest employee, I realized the prices were always $2.00 less than what the customer was charged. They rang up a $4.00 beer in the register, but it cost the customer $6.00, a $9.00 drink was rung up as $7.00, and so on. The former employees were skimming off the top. I had to put an end to it.

That next Tuesday, I'm bartending during the line dancing event and a man walks in. Literally moseying over to the bar, this 75, 80-year-old man wearing a cowboy hat, gives me a wink and a finger gun. "Are you the new owner?" I nodded yes. "How long you been doing this line dancing?" This was about to be a really good story or something bad, but I couldn't tell by his poker face. I relayed that we started about three months ago and did it weekly. He shakes his head in disbelief. Gary, a longtime resident of Lower Pottsgrove shares that he just discovered we had line dancing from our digital sign on High Street, also informing me that the sign was blinking too fast.

In my attempts to advertise, I didn't realize the default setting was set on one second intervals. Gary told me he drove around the block to get the details. Thanks to Gary, I quickly fixed the sign and slowed it down to four second adverts. We got to talking and Gary shared that when he was 10 years old, he and a friend were eating breakfast at the nearby Rosedale Diner, now a McDonald's. On this random morning, in walks Louie Armstrong who proceeds to buy their breakfast. He was a frequent performer back in the big band era and had played there the night before. Gary never forgot that and loves telling anyone who'll listen. Not having missed a Tuesday night since, whether he's sitting down or going round the dance floor, he's thrilled that The SunnyBrook Ballroom is once again being utilized and brought back to life.

People often share memories with me about SunnyBrook, and it's one of the things I like most about taking over the ballroom. We will never change the name. SunnyBrook has been around since 1931. The first thing built on that property was a circular swimming pool in 1926. Unlike pools of today where the deep end is near the edge of the pool, the deepest part of this pool was in the middle. The center, being thirty feet away and 15 feet deep, became a liability and was later filled in.

Subsequently, the ballroom was constructed in 1931. Among the many memories shared with me, most people have one of five: The pool being filled in in 1998, themselves or someone they knew getting married there, a prom, the big bands, or brunches with Ursula, a pipe organ from 1928 originally built for a one-room movie house in Lansdale, where it played the music and sound effects during the silent film era.

SunnyBrook started as a swim club for socialites, then with the addition of the ballroom hosted some of the most famous entertainers of the 30's and 40's. With the likes of Frank Sinatra, Louis Armstrong, Benny Goodman, and many more it was a premier hot spot in the country. There is a lot of history that comes with this compound, and I hope to continue the legacy.

Chapter 9 – Laying the Foundation

After planting my feet at The SunnyBrook Ballroom in Pottstown, PA, SoulJoel's has not only adjusted to the new space, new area, and new environment, we've also grown by introducing new interactive experiences to the community. I get more fulfillment from all the different events we do at SunnyBrook than ever before. We have had the biggest comedians in the world on stage here, and will continue to do so, but we've also been blessed and excited to give people even more reasons to come down the driveway. From weekly line dancing, monthly salsa, bachata, ballroom, and swing dancing to music events, drag brunches, charity events, bingo, weddings, proms, trivia, live music, and a regular psychic medium show, we have something for everyone!

In the quest to bolster my business and carry on with supplying quality entertainment, the many unique rooms at SunnyBrook are used simultaneously. For example, on Tuesdays we have line dancing in the ballroom and an open-mic night in the Melody Room. There might be 50 people line dancing and 50 people at the open mic, that's 100 people in the building on a Tuesday night. Both events have been thriving since we started in September of 2022. It's hectic, but holding multiple events on the same night also takes the financial pressure off a singular event, while offering a variety of options for the area.

Chuck Gulati, the former owner mentored me over the first year, describing what worked for him and how he ran the place. I also confided in Amy Daniels, the granddaughter of Ray Hartenstein Sr., the man who built SunnyBrook. Amy and I met at least every other month, sometimes once a month, to grab coffee or dinner. She shared with me what events were traditionally held at SunnyBrook and which ones were popular and profitable. These interactions brought back the extremely well-liked Easter and Mother's Day brunches, as well as a monthly event starring Ursula the pipe organ. Receiving that mentorship from the family who built the ballroom was invaluable to me, especially over that first, frantic year. Knowing that she approved of what we were achieving by bringing life back to this historic landmark, while preserving history, means a lot to my family and me.

In addition to ha-has and cha-chas, I started a podcast. Well, restarted, but this time I was going to interview comedians and other guests about the behind the scenes at SoulJoel's. Jesse Marchese, one of the comedians that helps run the open mics, came up to me and recommended it. I had done podcasts before, as I mentioned, but didn't currently have the time or the bandwidth to produce one. Jesse stepped up and now produces the *Bring 'Em Out!* podcast I co-host with Alan Hill. Jesse came up with the idea for the name, because not only do I bring out people to the shows, I bring out talent to the suburbs. 55,000 people over a 16-month period, from 27 different states, all during an international clusterfuck.

The first and only person I thought about co-hosting was Alan Hill. Alan and I met during the pandemic and became fast friends. His love for comedy rivals his love for music, having taught guitar for 25 years and currently part of the band Snapsquatch, a groove-based jam band. Anyone who has been to a SoulJoel comedy show has most likely seen, and almost definitely heard, Alan. With his boisterous laugh, huge smile under a distinctive white beard and ever-present Philadelphia Eagles jersey, he's a comic favorite. He was a perfect fit.

In February of 2023 we started the *'Bring 'Em Out!'* podcast. It comes out every Tuesday at noon. Fridays at noon, we added another weekly segment highlighting local businesses. Teaming up with them during the pandemic was one sure thing that helped us stay afloat. I interview a different, fellow entrepreneur, and we discuss various aspects of owning a business, locally and universally. You can check them both out on YOUTUBE.COM/@SOULJOELTV or wherever you get your podcasts.

Now, the challenge was to rebrand SoulJoel's to be recognized for more than just a one-of-a-kind outdoor comedy venue. On top of all the new, added events, we had reopened Gatsby's, naming it Gatsby's Pub, introducing a more relaxed vibe to the former high-end restaurant. We wanted a place where people could grab drinks and food before and after shows and for people from the neighborhood wanting to grab a meal or hang out at the bar. Again, I had to acclimatize myself to new rules and conditions. I went from a BYO business model in Royersford to a place with a liquor license. The need was to reprogram the public into understanding that, because of liability issues, we were no longer 'bring your own bottle'. As much as we advertise our restaurant and bar, we still get questions on social media asking if we can recommend a great place in the area to eat. Trying to get the word out has been challenging, but we will keep posting and advertising and, hopefully, soon BYO will become a fond memory.

One thing the public doesn't need help understanding is the genius of Date Attell. He returned to SoulJoel's, in 2023, for his first appearance at our Sunnybrook location. The hype was through the roof. He packed two sold-out shows in one night under the comedy dome. There is a special energy in the air when Dave is performing. Known as a comic's comic, there were 20 or 30 other comedians hanging in the back of the dome watching his set. Standing there, watching a master on stage and looking over the fellowship of fans who had all gathered at our new home, I felt like the dream I had envisioned years before was realized.

Besides being a brilliant comic, Dave Attell is also a kind-hearted, giving person. Normally, we're the ones supplying snacks and drinks for the talent, doing our best to make them feel comfortable, appreciated, and welcome. In turn, Dave, known for bringing candy wherever he's booked, arrived that night and handed me two bags of sweets to be given to the staff. He also has a knack for remembering any staff he works with, making a point to ask them specific questions based on conversations they had at his last show, often months later.

Speaking of snacks and amazing talent, Rachel Feinstein came in December of 2023 to run through her hour, preparing for her Netflix special taping later that week. When our staff asked her if there was anything she wanted to eat or drink before the show, she candidly replied, "I know this is going to sound ridiculous, but can you remove these snacks from the green room? I have to tape my Netflix special next week." This, of course, made everyone laugh. The staff removed the temptations from the room, and I only found out about this exchange as they were putting the snacks back the next day. To date, the funniest green room request we ever had.

As we continue to book the biggest acts and funniest people, they sometimes book us. In early 2023, Shuli Egar reached out wanting to do a live show of his podcast, *The Uncle Rico Show*. This unplanned, on-the-spot roast show, featured Shuli, The Reverend Bob Levy, and Mike Morse. The three of them would invite a bunch of other comedians and radio personalities for one big production. Much of time, they were comedians who had never been on a show together, mainly because they were from rival radio shows like Howard Stern and Opie and Anthony. This rare line-up saw fans from 30 different states. People were flying in from all across the nation - Florida to as far away as Washington State - calling us to check for the nearest airport. Flying in to attend a show at SoulJoel's was hard to wrap my head around.

Show day started off with High Pitch Erik, known for being a Howard Stern Wack Packer, enjoying cigar, looking at me and asking, "Is this a new place or the old place?" It struck me funny, because the only thing the old stove factory and Historic SunnyBrook Ballroom had in common were walls. Prior to show time, the crowd started chanting what sounded like "Jerry! Jerry!" from *The Jerry Springer Show*, but what they were really shouting was "Perry! Perry!" for Perry Caravello, who had starred in *Windy City Heat* and was one of the biggest personalities on the show. I wasn't familiar with Perry, but his dedicated followers were hardcore fans. I found out just how hardcore months later.

One of our patrons, who attends Thursday trivia night inside Gatsby's Pub, shared with me that he was a driver for DoorDash on the weekends. He recounts that earlier that year he dropped off a bag of McDonald's to the green room for one of the comedians and got yelled at. He was taken aback and rightfully so. Apparently, Perry Caravello hates McDonald's. His fans know this and will send him deliveries wherever he's performing, as a surprise. It drives him nuts each and every time.

Every room at SunnyBrook has its own purpose and feel, but can also be adjusted to each new adventure that presents itself. The Melody room for comedy, the ballroom for a variety of large events, Gatsby's Pub with trivia, live music and various other one-offs, and even the green room, each have their own vibe. It's a far cry from a wooden platform in a dirt lot, but no matter what has come our way, we made it work through blood, sweat, and tears and laughter, lots and lots of laughter. Along with the iconic dome, SoulJoel's at SunnyBrook has become a thriving complex of entertainment.

Not Funny – The Soul Behind Joel

Chapter 10 – Last, but Not Ceased

I love all the memories from the past three to four years. Drafting this book has helped me relive, remember, and rejoice in how far we have come here at SoulJoel's. Over the last few months, it's been a wild ride with all these stories popping up in my head at the strangest times, and I love carrying them with me as I look towards the future. I've seen how each decision, every worried hour, and all seemingly random signs, have connected to bring me where I am today, The SunnyBrook Ballroom, and I'm not alone. Many people have shared their favorite memories from all stages of SoulJoel's. One intertwines all the above, and it features the lovable Todd Barry.

Todd was getting ready for a new tour and, like most comedians at the time, came to SoulJoel's dome to run it. In the meantime, I had received a phone call from a mother who was bringing her son and future daughter-in-law to the show. She wanted to set up a fun way for her son to propose and put together the idea of him doing it at a show. (If you know Todd Barry, you might guess where this is headed.) Coincidentally, Todd was walking down the hill in Royersford, to the dome, at the same time as the mom, prior to the show. She got extremely excited and blurted out, "I'm looking forward to my son getting engaged at the show tonight!" Without skipping a beat, in true Todd fashion, he quipped back, "Not on my stage. Not at my show." It was priceless. Inside I was laughing, but also tormented. I want to make everyone happy, but I totally understood Todd's side.

We ended up waiting until the show was over, and during the standing ovation (Todd cruuuushed), while the crowd was still clapping, I went back to close the show. "Thank you for coming out! Follow us on Facebook and Instagram, we'll post pictures from tonight's show!" I glance at the couple in the front, "Looks like you guys had a good time. I believe he has something to say." and I handed him the ring box. He inevitably asked her to marry him, and she joyfully said yes. I ended with a smile, "Only at Soul Joel's!". ABP – always be plugging. I learned that from my parents, it's who I am and what I do. But it doesn't end there.

The same couple booked their wedding at SunnyBrook for September of 2022, one month prior to me taking over. They had no idea, nor did I, that Soul Joel's would be part of their engagement and their wedding. Since I was booking shows and in negotiations with the location, I was lucky enough to stop in at their wedding and wish them congratulations. It's events like these that I treasure. I help bring people together, create lifelong memories, and have a laugh at the same time.

SoulJoel's at SunnyBrook has had its trials and tribulations along with its successes and comforts. Bringing back the dome was a definite, but also a double-edged sword. The dome is what people associate with SoulJoel's. It is the symbol of outdoor comedy during the pandemic. Resurrecting the structure, not to mention spending the money to rebuy it, this time costing us $75,000, was a huge undertaking, but there was no question about whether or not we would. The dome was nonnegotiable. We continue to book outdoor shows from Labor Day to Memorial Day and will for the foreseeable future.

Managing a full-time bar and restaurant with four walls and indoor plumbing, coming from BYOB and porta-potties, was a welcome change, but brings its own set of obstacles and challenges. We are grateful to now have multiple rooms and can run big indoor shows as well, entertaining headliners year-round. The ballroom can sell 1,000 to 1,200 tickets a night, even doing two big shows a night. The Melody room holds up to 250, hosting a variety of shows and comics at all levels.

It's incredible to think that way back in 2020 in Royersford, Joey St. John, my sister and I set a goal to sell out one show Friday and one show Saturday, totaling eight shows for the whole month and bringing 1,200 people through the doors. When we came to SunnyBrook, we strove for at least 1,000 people a week. Only a year after taking over the ballroom, we've realized bringing 1,000 people in one day. From the goal of 1,200 a month to 1,000 a week to 1,000 in a day in four short, chaotic, unstable years felt like a lucid dream.

When we had Jim Breuer on the anniversary of SoulJoel's at SunnyBrook's opening, November 1, 2023, he played to 1,000 people two nights in a row, a Wednesday and Thursday for that matter. Just four years prior, we had one show over the weekend for a total of 150 people. I couldn't have imagined growing exponentially that fast in such a short amount of time.

On a suggestion by Alan Hill, we modeled the Melody Room, the main comedy room, after Robert Kelly's special *Killbox,* produced by Louis CK. In his special, he arranged the seating in three sections, surrounding the stage so that the comic is engulfed in laughter, hearing it from all sides.

We've had a lot of great feedback, and the comedians have loved it. There are also no interruptions, no check spots, no table service, and no minimums. Gatsby's Pub is adjacent, so patrons can eat and drink before or after the shows. It's 100% comedy during the shows, another thing comedians rave about.

If you have ever been to a show, you've heard my intro song, "Bring Em Out" by T.I. I've always used that song, but when we moved to SunnyBrook I had Cipha Sounds, a NYC DJ, "famous in New York" as he likes to proclaim, who had also worked on *Chappelle's Show,* and now does comedy, mix a special song for me. When we opened SoulJoel's in 2019, we played "Bring Em Out" beat matched into "Soul Man". It hyped people up, put them in a good mood, and ultimately trained the audiences to know that once they heard that song, the show was about to start.

This past year, we had Dave Attell for two shows inside the dome and one of the featured comedians noted that the audience went nuts when our song played. Not only were they there to see Dave, but they were also excited to be supporting me and local businesses. I had Cipha add Frank Sinatra's "My Way" leading into "Bring 'Em Out", and that's what plays at the start of every comedy show at SoulJoel's. I've talked about seeing signs throughout my journey. One of the songs that often played for my mom as she was driving was "My

Way". Combine that with the fact that Frank Sinatra performed with Jimmy Dorsey at SunnyBrook back in the big band era, well, there's my sign.

Prior to the shutdown, I had planned on booking music and comedy luncheons during the week, shows targeted mainly towards seniors and others who may not work during that time. COVID interrupted that idea until the spring of 2023 when Denny Frye, from the band The Sounds of SunnyBrook, called. Within an hour of him calling, we were sitting down with his niece, Jayne McHugh, and Donald Kuszyk discussing future dates.

Denny and Don shared memories of performing at SunnyBrook over the years. At 79 and 86 years old respectively, the two expressed the desire to bring back their status as the house band at SunnyBrook, as they once were from 2007 to 2016. Excited to work with them and fulfill my pre-COVID plans, The Sounds of SunnyBrook, a 17-piece band playing songs from Glenn Miller to Stan Kento, are periodically booked Wednesday afternoons from 1-3pm. Their next big appearance will be April 7th for a Sunday Swing Dance party.

When I took over SunnyBrook, a compound built in 1931 and the largest ballroom east of the Mississippi sprawling 14,000 square feet, the acoustics were not near what they are today. The room's floor and ceiling were built so that sound from the stage would travel to the way back. Microphones were just starting to be used to amplify voices in theaters and weren't considered during construction. Ten years ago, the owners sectioned off the Melody Room to start holding conferences and other such gatherings during the week. We continue to use each room with the audiences and performers in mind, wanting the best experience for everyone.

Looking back to one of the incidents that impacted our business, hosting our first ever Pride Event in 2021 brought some heat. We were the only venue holding a Pride event for the LGBTQ community in the greater Philadelphia area, due to the shutdown. It was held under the dome, and we swept network TV. NBC, CBS, and ABC all came to cover us. The funny thing was only ABC called us ahead of time, sending word that they were on their way. When I saw a reporter, I introduced myself, noted that they were from ABC and thanked them for showing up. She corrected me, identifying herself with CBS. My eyes were looking up at her eyes, and I hadn't noticed the logo on her chest, not even imagining there would be more than one reporter showing up that day to cover this event. It was overwhelming, to say the least. Our hard work was paying off, but it didn't come without controversy.

In 2022, when we were in between venues, we held a much smaller Pride event at the Colonial Theater in Phoenixville. This past year, we held our third annual event, *Pridezilla*, inside the SunnyBrook Ballroom. The event was fabulous. We had drag queens, various comedians, including Irene Tu from San Francisco, Jimbo from *RuPaul's Drag Race* (who, we found out after, won the eighth season of *RuPaul's Drag Race All Stars*), and Jessica Kirson headlining at night. Jessica has been headlining SoulJoel shows for years, dating back to the Valley Forge casino. Over the last couple of years, she has blown up on social media, and now she's doing theaters all over the country and internationally. She came back, selling over 300 tickets on a Sunday night to headline our third annual Pride Fest. It's so cool to watch and be a part of the growth of comedians, as I've seen comedians go from open-micer to national headliner.

The photographer for this event, Lauren Ariel, delivered the pictures about five days after, and we instantly posted them on our socials. Straight away the negative comments started. How could we have drag queens at their beloved SunnyBrook? It was a ticketed event, for 18 and older, not free at the library. Five hundred tickets were sold that day with Jessica headlining the finale to 300 people, 150 of which were sold to straight couples. It wasn't just the LGBTQ community in attendance, it was people from all walks of life coming out to have a fun time.

As I mentioned, we strive to give people a different reason to come down our driveway and always have. Entertainment six days a week, no matter what it is. We ended up getting one star Google reviews stating that SoulJoel's at SunnyBrook was hosting immoral drag shows. Well, I ended up sharing that and telling our loyal fans, and from those two one-star Google reviews, we ended up getting over 1,000 five-star reviews in seven days. We hadn't even had 500 total reviews up until that point. It was utterly amazing.

Over 2020 and 2021, SoulJoel's raised over $35,000 for local charities and nonprofit organizations, always donating half of the money from our comedy shows on Thursday nights. Even during our transition from Royersford to Pottstown, we raised over $5000. This is something that SoulJoel's hangs our hat on, and we are immensely proud of raising money through laughter. There is no better night out.

One of the Fundraisers we hosted at Westover during the transition was for Branden Sisca, a state trooper and chief of the Trappe Fire Company in Montgomery County who was tragically struck on 95 by a drunk driver. I was approached to raise money for his family, as his wife was pregnant and expecting their first child. We raised $5000 for them.

About a month or so after, I was in the SoulJoel Mobile, driving around town. I often get recognized by people who will take pictures if they see my car. This one particular day I was on Egypt Road, right by where it intersects with 422. A guy next to me at the light on his cell phone rolls down the window, puts his cell phone on his shoulder and shouts, "Hey, are you SoulJoel?" Which instantly makes me laugh, as if I have an entire fleet of vehicles, but in fact mine is the only one and I'm always the one driving it. I told him I was, and he went on to introduce himself as Branden's uncle and thanked me for what we did for his family and the surrounding community.

As he was telling me all of this, the light had already turned green. Lots of horns were honking behind us, and he started yelling, "Hold on a second! Hold on a second!" I'm having mixed emotions, part of me is panicking because of the line of cars behind me, but another part is embracing this moment. As I'm grinding and working hard, whether it be through the pandemic, acquiring a new location, raking sand, or filling up the calendar, I never take time to reflect on what has transpired, what we've accomplished, or how far we have come until I get affirmation like this and see how our shows impact lives. So, thank you, all of you, for helping make my dream come true.

In hindsight, I can now see that all roads have led to the historic SunnyBrook Ballroom. We were meant to take over this property. Sometimes it's hard to see what will be when you're going through it. As we were in the middle of leaving Royersford, I just wanted to have a permanent home, but patience isn't my strong suit and time is not something that I had.

My mom spoke to me, the way she spoke to all her clients. "When you find the home, you're supposed to be in, you will know." At the time, I didn't want to hear it and was anxious to know what God had planned for me. After every other deal fell apart and all doors appeared to be closing, I was, though it may seem strange, being steered in the right direction. I'm not 100% sure what will happen in the future, who is? But I will continue to work ceaselessly, listen to the people I trust, follow the signs, and always bring 'em out!

Afterword

I've set some new goals in my life, now. Providing quality, exciting, fun entertainment will always be my main goal, but my sights are set on even bigger things for SunnyBrook. Look out for a complete renovation of the upstairs room, which will provide yet another place to hold shows, weddings, proms, and some new events that are in the works. We will be able to fill the new room with 400 to 500 people and plan on hosting big-time music acts, lots of comedy, film festivals and more!

Joel Richardson and Lu

Made in the USA
Columbia, SC
25 March 2024

a364b032-7dfa-4dad-942b-fc1aa7f952aaR01